TRADE BARRIERS IN EUROPE

HF2033 .T73 2007

0134111 588 510

Trade barriers in Europe

c2007.

TRADE BARRIERS IN EUROPE

PAULA R. LIGNELLI
EDITOR

Nova Science Publishers, Inc.
New York

Copyright © 2007 by Nova Science Publishers, Inc.

All rights reserved. No part of this book may be reproduced, stored in a retrieval system or transmitted in any form or by any means: electronic, electrostatic, magnetic, tape, mechanical photocopying, recording or otherwise without the written permission of the Publisher.

For permission to use material from this book please contact us:
Telephone 631-231-7269; Fax 631-231-8175
Web Site: http://www.novapublishers.com

NOTICE TO THE READER

The Publisher has taken reasonable care in the preparation of this book, but makes no expressed or implied warranty of any kind and assumes no responsibility for any errors or omissions. No liability is assumed for incidental or consequential damages in connection with or arising out of information contained in this book. The Publisher shall not be liable for any special, consequential, or exemplary damages resulting, in whole or in part, from the readers' use of, or reliance upon, this material.

Independent verification should be sought for any data, advice or recommendations contained in this book. In addition, no responsibility is assumed by the publisher for any injury and/or damage to persons or property arising from any methods, products, instructions, ideas or otherwise contained in this publication.

This publication is designed to provide accurate and authoritative information with regard to the subject matter covered herein. It is sold with the clear understanding that the Publisher is not engaged in rendering legal or any other professional services. If legal or any other expert assistance is required, the services of a competent person should be sought. FROM A DECLARATION OF PARTICIPANTS JOINTLY ADOPTED BY A COMMITTEE OF THE AMERICAN BAR ASSOCIATION AND A COMMITTEE OF PUBLISHERS.

LIBRARY OF CONGRESS CATALOGING-IN-PUBLICATION DATA

Trade barriers in Europe / Paula R. Lignelli (editor).
  p. cm.
 Includes index.
 ISBN-13: 978-1-60021-956-6
 ISBN-10: 1-60021-956-X
 1. Europe--Commercial policy. 2. Foreign trade regulation--Europe. I. Peltz, Marlene C.
HF2033.T73 2008
382'.73094--dc22
                      2007033702

Published by Nova Science Publishers, Inc. ✣ *New York*

CONTENTS

Preface		vii
Chapter 1	European Union	1
Chapter 2	Kenya	59
Chapter 3	Norway	69
Chapter 4	Russia	79
Chapter 5	Switzerland	99
Chapter 6	Turkey	107
Chapter 7	Ukraine	115
Chapter 8	Uzbekistan	129
Index		137

PREFACE

A trade barrier is a general term that describes any government policy or regulation that restricts international trade. The barriers can take many forms, including Import duties, Import licenses, Export licenses, Import quotas, Tariffs, and Subsidies. Non-tariff barriers to trade, Voluntary Export Restraints, and Local Content Requirements. Most trade barriers work on the same principle: the imposition of some sort of cost on trade that raises the price of the traded products. If two or more nations repeatedly use trade barriers against each other, then a trade war results.

Economists generally agree that trade barriers are detrimental and decrease overall economic efficiency, this can be explained by the theory of comparative advantage. In theory, free trade involves the removal of all such barriers, except perhaps those considered necessary for health or national security. In practice, however, even those countries promoting free trade heavily subsidize certain industries, such as agriculture and steel. Examples of free trade areas are: North American Free Trade Agreement (NAFTA), South Asia Free Trade Agreement (SAFTA), European Free Trade Association, European Union (EU), Union of South American Nations. Other trade barriers include differences in culture, customs, traditions, laws, language and currency.

This book is based on information from the Office of the United States Trade Representative (USTR).

In: Trade Barriers in Europe
Editor: Paula R. Lignelli, pp. 1-58

ISBN: 978-1-60021-956-6
© 2007 Nova Science Publishers, Inc.

Chapter 1

EUROPEAN UNION

TRADE SUMMARY

The U.S. goods trade deficit with European Union was $116.6 billion in 2006, a decrease of $5.7 billion from $122.3 billion in 2005. U.S. goods exports in 2006 were $214.0 billion, up 14.8 percent from the previous year. Corresponding U.S. imports from European Union were $330.6 billion, up 7.1 percent. European Union countries, together, rank 2nd behind Canada as an export market for the United States in 2006.

U.S. exports of private commercial services (i.e., excluding military and government) to the European Union were $127.8 billion in 2005 (latest data available), and U.S. imports were $105.9 million. Sales of services in the European Union by majority U.S.-owned affiliates were $249.1 billion in 2004 (latest data available), while sales of services in the United States by majority European Union owned firms were $224.3 billion.

The stock of U.S. foreign direct investment (FDI) in the European Union in 2005 was $949.0 billion (latest data available), down from $973.0 billion in 2004. U.S. FDI in the European Union is concentrated largely in the non-bank holding companies, manufacturing, finance, and wholesale trade sectors.

OVERVIEW

In most respects, the enormous United States-EU trade and investment relationship operates smoothly and to the great benefit of companies, workers, and consumers on both sides of the Atlantic. In recognition of this fact, leaders of the United States and the European Union agreed, in the context of the June 2005 United States-EU Summit (reaffirmed at the June 2006 United States-EU Summit), to pursue additional transatlantic economic integration through a series of cooperative initiatives in areas such as regulatory cooperation, intellectual property rights enforcement, innovation, and trade and security, among other issues.

Despite the broadly positive nature of the United States-EU trade and investment relationship, U.S. exporters in some sectors continue to face chronic barriers to entering the EU market. A number of these barriers have been highlighted in this report for many years, despite repeated efforts to resolve them through bilateral consultations or, in some cases, the dispute settlement provisions of the WTO.

Over the course of the past year, U.S. concerns continued regarding the EU's longstanding policy of subsidizing the development, production, and marketing of large civil aircraft. In general, barriers to access for U.S. agricultural exports continue to be a source of frustration for the United States. Even where formal EU agricultural tariff barriers may be relatively low, U.S. exports of leading commodities such as corn, beef, poultry, soy, pork and rice are significantly restricted or excluded altogether due to restrictive EU non-tariff barriers or regulatory approaches that often do not reflect a sound assessment of actual risks posed by the goods in question. In addition, the trade-distorting effects of various EU Member State policies governing pharmaceuticals and health care products are generating concerns related both to market access and to healthcare innovation. This year's report also outlines concerns of U.S. exporters with respect to a number of emerging EU policies that may threaten to disrupt trade in the future, such as the proposed new EU chemicals regulation.

On October 17, 2006, the EU Council approved Romania and Bulgaria's accession to the European Union, and the two countries joined the EU on January 1, 2007. Because Romania and Bulgaria began adopting EU laws and regulations in the lead-up to their accession to the EU, this report includes a discussion of enlargement-related trade policy issues as well as other barriers in the Romanian and Bulgarian markets.

IMPORT POLICIES

Customs Administration

Notwithstanding the existence of a body of EU customs law, the EU does not operate as a single customs administration. Rather, there is a separate agency responsible for the administration of EU customs law in each of the EU's 27 Member States. The 27 separate agencies do not administer EU customs law in a uniform manner, as is required by Article X:3(a) of the General Agreement on Tariffs and Trade 1994 ("GATT 1994"). No EU institutions or procedures ensure that EU rules on classification, valuation, origin, and customs procedures are applied in a way that remains the same from Member State to Member State. Moreover, no EU rules require the customs agency in one Member State to follow the decisions of the customs agency in another Member State with respect to materially identical issues.

On some questions, where the customs agencies in different Member States administer EU law differently, the matter may be referred to the Customs Code Committee. The Committee is an entity established by the Community Customs Code to assist the European Commission. The Committee consists of representatives of the Member States and is chaired by a representative of the Commission. While, in theory, the Committee exists to help reconcile differences among Member State practices and thereby help to achieve uniformity of administration, in practice its success in this regard has been limited.

Not only are the Committee and other EU-level institutions ineffective tools for achieving the uniform administration of EU customs law, but the EU also lacks tribunals or procedures for the prompt review and EU-wide correction of administrative actions relating to customs matters. Instead, review is provided separately by each Member State's tribunals – and rules regarding these reviews can vary from Member State to Member State. Thus, a trader encountering non-uniform administration of EU customs law in multiple Member States must bring a separate appeal in each Member State whose agency rendered an adverse decision. Ultimately, a question of interpretation of EU law may be referred to the Court of Justice of the European Union (ECJ). The judgments of the ECJ have effect throughout the EU. However, referral of questions to the ECJ generally is discretionary and ECJ proceedings can take years. Thus, obtaining corrections with EU-wide effect for administrative actions relating to customs matters is a cumbersome and frequently time-consuming process.

The United States has raised both of the foregoing sets of concerns with the EU in various fora. The concerns have taken on new prominence in light of the expansion of the EU (which now includes 27 Member States) and the focus of the Doha Development Agenda on trade facilitation. Given the growing negative consequences of deficiencies in the EU's customs administration and review procedures, the United States initiated WTO consultations in September 2004. Subsequently, in March 2005, a dispute settlement panel was formed to consider U.S. complaints.

On June 16, 2006, the panel circulated its report, in which it found a lack of uniform administration in certain specified instances, and found no breach of the EU's obligations with respect to prompt review and correction of customs determinations. The United States and EU each appealed different aspects of the panel report. In its report issued on November 13, 2006, the Appellate Body agreed that the panel had misread the U.S. complaint. The Appellate Body also agreed with the United States on certain other legal points and agreed with the EU that the panel had erred in finding non-uniform administration in two particular instances. Finally, the Appellate Body agreed with the panel's finding of no breach of the EU's obligation regarding prompt review and correction of customs administrative action.

The panel and Appellate Body reports were adopted at the December 11, 2006 meeting of the WTO Dispute Settlement Body. The reports as adopted included a finding that the EU is in breach of its obligation of uniform administration with respect to rules pertaining to the tariff classification of certain liquid crystal display monitors.

EU Enlargement

In anticipation of the accession of Romania and Bulgaria to the EU on January 1, 2007, the United States in December 2006 entered into negotiations with the EU within the framework of GATT provisions relating to the expansion of customs unions. Upon their accessions, Romania and Bulgaria were required to change their tariff schedules to conform to the EU's common external tariff schedule, resulting in increased tariffs on certain products imported into Romania and Bulgaria from third countries. Under General Agreement on Tariffs and Trade 1994 (GATT 1994) Articles XXIV: 6 and XXVIII, the United States is entitled to compensation from the EU to offset some of these changes. The expansion of pre-existing EU quotas to account for the addition of Romania and Bulgaria to the European Union common market is another key element of the negotiations. This round of enlargement presents particular issues for exporters to Romania and Bulgaria of key commodities such as pork, which will face a significant increase in applied tariff rates and the imposition of quotas. In 2007, the United States will seek to conclude an appropriate bilateral compensation agreement with the European Commission and ensure that its benefits are implemented as soon as possible.

On March 22, 2006, the United States and the EU signed a bilateral agreement within the framework of the GATT related to the May 2004 enlargement of the European Union. As part of the agreement, the EU opened new country-specific tariff-rate quotas for U.S. exports of boneless ham, poultry, and corn gluten meal. It expanded existing global tariff-rate Quotas for food preparations, fructose, pork, rice, barley, wheat, maize, preserved fruits, fruit juices, pasta, chocolate, pet food, beef, poultry, live bovine animals and sheep, and various cheeses and vegetables. It permanently reduced tariffs on protein concentrates, fish (hake, Alaska Pollack, surimi), chemicals (polyvinyl butyral), aluminum tube, and molybdenuym wire. These unilateral EU concessions went into effect in July 2006.

In addition to tariff changes, the adoption of EU non-tariff barriers by acceding member states has resulted in the loss of significant markets for U.S. exports of poultry, and severely restricted U.S. exports of other agricultural commodities (see Sanitary and Phytosanitary section).

In 2003, to address potential incompatibilities between Bilateral Investment Treaty (BIT) obligations and EU law, the United States and Romania and Bulgaria agreed to make several narrow amendments to the texts of their respective BITs. Both the United States and these two countries have ratified the BIT amendments, and the amendments entered into force upon an exchange of instruments. This exchange took place in Bulgaria on January 16, 2007, and in Romania on February 9.

The customs administration issues noted above for the EU will only become more complex with the addition of Romania and Bulgaria. In Bulgaria, in particular, exporters have reported inconsistent customs valuation and the use of minimum import prices, which may be applied arbitrarily to calculate customs duties.

WTO Information Technology Agreement

The United States has expressed concerns about EU proposals to apply duties as high as 14 percent to imports of several technologically-sophisticated versions of products covered under the WTO Information Technology Agreement (ITA). Such products include certain set-top boxes with a communication function (e.g. cable boxes), flat panel displays for computers, digital still image video cameras, and certain units of automatic data processing machines (e.g. multifunction or "all-in-one" printer/copier/scanner devices). All ITA Members, including the EU, committed to bind and eliminate customs duties on these products when coverage for the ITA was finalized in 1996. However, the EU continued to draft proposals in 2006 that would redefine what products are eligible for duty-free treatment, limiting such treatment to less technologically sophisticated versions of these products, many of which are no longer sold in today's marketplace. These new product definitions proposed by the EU are not found in the ITA and are so narrow that almost none of today's models of the aforementioned ITA products would be guaranteed duty-free treatment if imported into the EU. The United States has raised its concerns both bilaterally and in the ITA Committee in Geneva and will continue to press the EU to abide by the letter and spirit of the ITA.

Restrictions Affecting U.S. Wine Exports

Since the mid-1980s, U.S. wines have been permitted entry to the EU market through temporary exemptions from certain EU wine regulations governing permissible wine-making practices. The temporary nature of these derogations created continuous uncertainty for U.S. wine exporters. In 2002, the EU adopted a new wine labeling regulation (Commission Regulation No. 753/2002). The United States, along with a number of other WTO Members, raised serious concerns about the lack of clarity in the new regulation and its WTO-consistency and urged the EU to withdraw the regulation. The regulation appeared to be more trade restrictive than necessary to meet any legitimate objective, as it would prohibit the presentation on imported wine of information important for the marketing of wine unless certain conditions were met (e.g., the marketing information used must be regulated in the producing country). In addition, the EU imposed restrictions on the use of traditional terms listed in the regulation, in some instances granting exclusive use of a term to an EU wine, thereby raising national treatment concerns. Traditional terms are, for the most part, terms used with certain other expressions (often geographical indications) to describe wine or liqueur and in many cases the terms are merely descriptive (e.g., "ruby" and "tawny").

On March 10, 2006, the European Union and the United States signed an agreement on certain aspects of wine trade as a first phase to a broader agreement on trade in wine. The agreement, which went into effect the day of the signing, is intended to eliminate the uncertainties caused by the previous temporary exemptions and to provide more stable market conditions for the wine sector. The pact simplifies export procedures for American winemakers hoping to increase their share of a trade currently worth around $2.8 billion annually. It provides for mutual acceptance of current wine-making practices and sets up a consultative process for accepting new wine-making practices. It also addresses some of the concerns raised by the EU's wine-labeling regulation, including a provision for the use of certain EU-regulated terms on U.S. wine. Finally, the agreement provides for the negotiation of an additional agreement to further facilitate trade in wine between the parties. These negotiations began in June 2006.

Bananas

Acting against the backdrop of understandings reached separately with the United States and Ecuador in 2001 setting out the means for reaching a resolution to the long-running dispute regarding trade in bananas, the EU instituted a new banana import regime on January 1, 2006. The 2001 understandings required that by January 1, 2006, the EU must put in place a tariff-only regime for bananas. The understandings further required the EU to seek waivers of its GATT Article I and XIII obligations in order to continue temporarily a modified banana import regime incorporating tariff-rate quotas and import licensing requirements. The Article I waiver as finally granted by the WTO required that the future tariff-only regime result in at least maintaining total market access for MFN banana suppliers.

In the fall of 2005, the EU made two proposals for a new tariff rate for bananas. Both of these proposals were subject to review by a WTO arbitrator (according to the terms of the Article I waiver), which found that both proposals failed to satisfy the EU's obligation at least to maintain total market access for non-preferential suppliers of bananas to the EU market.

EU consultations and negotiations with a number of Latin American banana exporting countries throughout 2005 yielded no agreement on the shape of the EC's post-January 1, 2006 regime. The regime as eventually implemented on January 1, 2006, combined a 176 euro/metric ton most-favored nation (MFN) tariff level with a continued zero duty tariff-rate quota for bananas originating in Africa, Pacific and Caribbean (ACP) countries, with whom the EU maintains a preferential trading relationship. In November 2006, after continued negotiations failed to achieve a satisfactory result, Ecuador filed a request under Article 21.5 of the WTO Dispute Settlement Understanding for consultations with the EU regarding the compliance of this new regime with the EU's obligations under the WTO. The United States joined as a third party in these consultations.

The United States' strong interest is that the EU's import regime must uphold the EU's multilateral commitment to put in place a WTO-compatible structure that at least maintains total market access for non-preferential banana suppliers. While the United States does not directly export bananas to the EU, this is an issue of considerable importance to U.S. companies involved in the production, distribution, and marketing of bananas.

Market Access Restrictions for U.S. Pharmaceuticals

U.S. pharmaceutical companies encounter persistent market access problems throughout countries of the European Union due to the effective price, volume, and access controls placed on medicines by national governments. In most cases, Member State governments administer medicine reimbursement programs as part of their healthcare programs, which cover a significant segment of the market. The procedures for getting a product on the reimbursement list and the price controls maintained for those products that are on the list lack transparency and have a strong negative impact on U.S. exports. The EU also places strict controls on the nature of information that pharmaceutical companies can furnish to patients. The combination of these measures can limit patients' access to innovative products and may diminish investments by EU companies in pharmaceuticals research and development.

The EU's single market allows pharmaceuticals, like other goods, to move freely within the EU, while Member States' controlled prices vary greatly from one country to another. This situation permits intermediaries to buy medicines, often in bulk quantities, in EU countries where the government-determined price is lower and sell them in other EU countries where the price is set at a higher level – a practice known as parallel trade, where traders do not contribute any value to research and development costs.

Austria

Austria maintains a bureaucratic pharmaceutical reimbursement approval process that limits market access for innovative products. A pharmaceutical firm seeking to include a product on the list of reimbursable drugs without prior authorization must first obtain the approval of the umbrella organization of social insurance funds (Hauptverband/HVB). Almost all new innovative pharmaceuticals must be individually approved by HVB physicians, who remain reluctant to prescribe them to avoid bureaucratic hurdles. A reform of the reimbursement system came into effect on January 1, 2005, but the situation has not improved. U.S. companies operating in Austria report cumulative losses between $25 million and $100 million due to these practices.

Belgium

Pharmaceutical companies consider Belgium among the most inhospitable markets in Europe. Taxes, pricing policies, and slow approvals discourage investment in research and development. Prices on pharmaceuticals reimbursed through the Belgian healthcare system remain at well below European averages, and there is strong government pressure on doctors to favor generics and lowest-cost drugs over patented products. Further, in addition to the turnover and profit taxes applied exclusively in this sector, pharmaceutical companies are required to fund a buffer to cover what have been chronic gaps between budgeted and actual government spending on pharmaceuticals. In combination, these tax measures amount to a 10 percent to 11 percent additional levy on the sector. The government did not pass promised legislation in 2006 to exempt drugs under patent from a mandatory price decrease that went into effect in the fall of 2005.

Bulgaria

The Bulgarian government's drug supply mechanism constitutes a major market access barrier to U.S. pharmaceutical exports. New drug legislation imposes liability on companies for failures of distributors to meet drug supply obligations (incorrect or late deliveries). Instead of holding distributors accountable for correct distribution, the government holds pharmaceutical manufacturers liable for the distributors' performance, over which manufacturers have no control. The registration processes for pharmaceutical products and for drug pricing and reimbursement, including the process by which the National Health Insurance Fund classifies drugs, are cumbersome and non-transparent. Newer drugs are often arbitrarily classified with their older, generic versions for pricing purposes, thereby limiting companies' ability to recover their research and development costs.

Cyprus

The Cypriot pharmaceuticals market suffers from several distortions that have resulted in unnecessary barriers to trade and retail shortages of many pharmaceuticals. Of the 3,300 drugs sold in Cyprus prior to May 1, 2004, only around 2000 were available in October 2006.

Since acceding to the EU on May 1, 2004, the government of Cyprus (GOC) imposed retail price cuts for pharmaceuticals of around 20 percent. The mechanism used by the GOC to set pharmaceutical retail prices involves using a basket of prices of the same drug in eight other EU countries (identified as two high price, four medium price, and two low price countries). However, local representatives of pharmaceutical companies believe the selected countries are not representative, pushing the benchmark price downward. During 2006, the situation improved somewhat, with marginal price concessions to pharmaceutical importers.

Furthermore, the government discriminates against new, innovative drugs when procuring pharmaceuticals for the public health sector. Innovative, cutting-edge drugs are generally left off the government's procurement list until cheaper substitutes become available. Cyprus is currently overhauling its national health scheme, aiming to upgrade public health care by 2008. The process may result in reforms to the current government procurement system.

Czech Republic

In October 2005, the European Commission sent a letter initiating infringement proceedings against the government of the Czech Republic for not properly implementing the EU Transparency Directive. The complaint focused on the non-transparent pharmaceutical categorization process that decides which medicines will be covered by public health insurance and determines the level of reimbursement. In October 2006, the EC alerted the GOCR that they would move toward potential legal action unless the GOCR corrects this lack of transparency. The GOCR has drafted a legislative plan in consultation with industry and the EC to address the issue.

Denmark

The pharmaceutical industry, in general, and U.S. firms in particular, complain that Danish reimbursement standards lack objective and verifiable criteria and do not meet even minimal standards of transparency. Furthermore, the industry claims that the Danish government has failed to provide reimbursement for new innovative medicines or has delayed reimbursement for long periods. Within the context of the Danish social security system, this has the practical effect of preventing the sale and use of such medicines. The government has maintained pressure to further decrease prices or sales of innovative pharmaceutical products, and as of April 1, 2005, a new reimbursement system was introduced. Under the new rules, reimbursements are determined on the basis of the lowest-priced medicine available in each therapeutic category, meaning that the patients' own contributions increase unless the cheapest product (often generics) is chosen. Reimbursements only apply to medicines bought in a Danish-authorized pharmacy.

Finland

Innovative pharmaceutical companies in Finland have raised concerns that government regulations have resulted in an uncompetitive environment marked by pricing policies that place low ceilings on pharmaceutical prices and limit the price differentials allowed between generic and innovative products. Further, industry claims that it takes more than three years for a pharmaceutical product to be approved for full reimbursement under the national insurance scheme.

In early 2004, Finland's Ministry of Social Affairs and Health (MoSAH) began preparing legislation that would extend the time that brand-name drugs are protected from competition by generic alternatives. Research-based pharmaceutical companies, legislators and civil servants at MoSAH and the Ministry of Trade and Industry worked closely together and produced a report to the Minister of Social Affairs and Health. Parliament approved an amendment to the Finnish Medicine Act in late 2005 that prevents the inclusion of patent-infringing generic pharmaceuticals on national mandatory generic substitution lists. This amendment entered into effect on February 1, 2006.

France

France's new Health High Authority, HAS ("Haute Autorite de Sante"), an advisory body set up by the French government to spur French healthcare reform, began its activities on January 1, 2005. HAS plays a critical role in assessing the expected or actual clinical benefit delivered by healthcare products, procedures and services, and advises on decisions about inclusion of a product, medical device, health technology or procedure on the list of products and services that qualify for reimbursement under the French Social Security system. Since its inception, HAS has recommended that 221 drugs be removed from the list of reimbursable drugs. In spite of complaints from pharmaceutical companies, the new agency confirmed that France would maintain its own, separate assessment of innovative drugs, even after these products have been granted a Marketing Authorization under the Centralized European Procedure. HAS notes that the specific features of the French healthcare environment will have to be taken into account but that France intends, where possible, to initiate a strategy of alliances with other similar healthcare bodies in the EU.

Germany

As part of a broader health-care reform package, Germany introduced a reference pricing scheme on generic and patented pharmaceuticals on January 1, 2005. U.S. firms contend that they bear the brunt of cost-containment by virtue of their dominance (25 percent) of the German market. U.S. pharmaceutical companies note serious concerns about lack of transparency and fairness in the decision-making process related to the new reference pricing scheme, which does not provide a fair rate of return for patented, innovative medicines. Additional cost constraint measures were imposed through the combining of patented, innovative products with generic products, known as "jumbo groups." Both reference pricing and its variant, jumbo groups, are strongly opposed by U.S. pharmaceutical companies. The U.S. Government has raised this issue repeatedly with the German government, including during the visits of interagency U.S. health policy delegations to Berlin in June 2005 and February 2006. Legislation that went into effect in May 2006 clarified how drugs are declared innovative and provided more transparency in the decision-making process, addressing some industry concerns. The German government has continued to debate new, broader healthcare reform legislation, but the packages put forward to date have not contained further measures that would alleviate the disadvantages to U.S. and other countries' producers of innovative pharmaceuticals.

Hungary

In June 2004, the Hungarian government and various pharmaceutical companies signed a contract to end price freezes until December 31, 2006 and return drug prices to March 2004 levels. In addition, a draft document by the State Reform Committee suggests that healthcare spending could remain at current levels until 2010, in effect extending a June 2004 agreement that limits health budget increases to 5 percent. This measure, in conjunction with an October 2005 cap on company payments to the health budget, could have negative results for drug manufacturers, since current regulations state that pharmaceutical companies are responsible for financing gaps in the drug subsidy budget. Finally, the government of Hungary initiated a generic drug program in June 2005 encouraging doctors to prescribe alternatives to the name brands as part of its "100 steps" program.

Italy

U.S. companies have raised concerns about Italian government measures that they believe will have a deleterious impact on their business and could have a negative impact on patient care. Among these are: (i) an across-the-board decrease in reimbursement prices for almost 300 drugs now on the reimbursement list; (ii) an increase in the amount that industry must "pay back" to the central government for regions' annualized overspending on pharmaceuticals; and (iii) additional discounts on certain classes of drugs that will disproportionately disadvantage U.S. research-based companies. U.S. companies are eager to continue a dialogue with the Italian government to improve transparency in Italy's cost-containment measures and look for solutions that provide the greatest value in terms of potentially lifesaving innovation and patient care.

Lithuania

Some pharmaceutical products in Lithuania are sold at very low prices to consumers. The government reimburses pharmaceutical manufacturers the difference between this price and a price set by the health insurance law. The Lithuanian government amended this law on July 5, 2005, to change the formula used to calculate this price. The new formula yields a price that is 5 percent less than the average price of the drug in six Central and Eastern European countries. Pharmaceutical manufacturers are not required to participate in this system, and outside of this system, they are free to market their products and charge market prices.

The Netherlands

The Dutch Ministry of Health views pharmaceuticals as a prime target for savings in its national healthcare budget. Industry asserts that the Ministry does not fully recognize the added value of incremental innovation. Various measures are in force or planned that delay the reimbursement of new compounds or favor generic drugs. The current multi-party agreement between the Ministry of Health, insurers, pharmacists, and generic manufacturers was extended for another year in 2005. Nefarma, the association representing the innovative industry, joined the agreement on January 1, 2005. Under the current agreement, Nefarma members will reduce their prices of multi-source brands (out-of-patent products for which there are generics available) by an average of 40 percent. This reduction affects older products, while new, innovative products are protected. Discussions among the same stakeholders now have the objective of either extending the multi-party agreement after the end of 2007 or to modernize the current reimbursement system and/or the Pharmaceutical Pricing Act.

Poland

For several years, the Polish government has alleged that foreign pharmaceutical companies charged excessive margins for drugs and owed hundreds of millions of dollars in fines under a 2000-2002 ordinance related to pharmaceutical pricing. Although this ordinance was subsequently struck down by Polish courts, the issue remains unsettled and subject to potential legal action by both the National Health Fund and Finance Ministry. Poland has thus far ignored requests for EU arbitration of this issue. The uncertainty and amount of the potential fines threaten not only future investment, but also the existing investments of foreign innovative pharmaceutical firms in Poland.

In July 2006, the Polish government instituted a 13 percent across-the-board price cut on all imported pharmaceutical products. The Polish government contended that it cut prices in response to exchange rate changes. According to the U.S. pharmaceutical industry, however, the Polish government makes reimbursements in Polish zloty and should therefore be unaffected by exchange rate variations. The pharmaceutical industry has also raised questions of WTO-consistency, on the grounds that the regulation applies only to importers. The European Commission is investigating the consistency of the price reductions with EU rules.

In September 2006, some foreign pharmaceutical companies were issued additional price reductions to hospital supply products ranging from 4 percent to 34 percent that entered into effect in early October 2006. No explanation was given for the reductions.

Polish legislation requires that the Ministry of Health update its drug reimbursement list at least once a year. It is from this list that doctors most often prescribe drugs as purchases are subsidized by the Polish National Health Fund, making them more affordable for patients. In the seven years prior to December 2006, the Polish Ministry of Health added only four innovative drugs to its reimbursement list. Failure to add drugs to the reimbursement list seriously undermined U.S. and international innovative drug producers' market position in favor of the Polish generic industry. In December of 2006, the Health Ministry added 12 new innovative drugs to its reimbursement list (comprising over 50 products). The Polish government announced that it plans to add another 20 innovative drugs (comprising over 100 products) to the list in Summer 2007. The U.S. pharmaceutical industry is concerned that reimbursement prices are set arbitrarily and often without transparency. Pending legislation will require the Health Ministry to publish its selection criteria and formalize an appeals process for drugs not selected for the reimbursement list.

Portugal

In September 2006, Portugal enacted the Consumption of Medicine in Hospitals statute, an adaptation of EU Directive 2004/27/EC. The statute restricts the introduction of new medicines in hospitals, with the exception of generics, by requiring studies demonstrating that the new drugs are more cost effective than the generic versions. An individual study can cost up to $50,000 and take one year to complete. This restriction already existed for new entries in the retail sector. Industry estimates that these requirements will result in a cost to U.S. firms of $315,000 in studies and $12.6 million in lost sales.

Pharmaceuticals destined for retail and hospital use have been given 0 percent and 4 percent growth ceilings, respectively. If the pharmaceutical industry surpasses these percentages, it will be required to repay the government the overage, not to exceed $30 million and $15 million, respectively.

Substantial delays in government payments to the pharmaceutical industry persist although the government's outstanding debt has decreased from $1 billion in 2005 to $883 million in 2006.

Spain

A pharmaceutical must go through a lengthy and costly approval and registration process with the Spanish Ministry of Health unless it was previously registered in another EU Member State or with the European Medicines Agency. This process delays the entry of innovative pharmaceuticals into the Spanish market. Further delays are caused by a lengthy administrative pricing process, coupled with onerous government reimbursement procedures.

Slovakia

U.S. and European pharmaceutical companies complain that a Slovakian Ministry of Health decree (No. 723/2004), which went into effect on October 15, 2005, further reduces the transparency of government decisions regarding the pricing and reimbursement decisions for medicines prescribed by national health insurance. The decree specifies the rules to be applied in determining the price of the medicinal product and level of reimbursement. The original decree provided detailed rules for the calculation of the price and the level of reimbursement. However, recent amendment of the decree cancelled the detailed rules for determining the reimbursement amount and, instead, provided the Ministry of Health, as the deciding authority, with wide discretion to decide on the amount of reimbursement without setting a clear set of guidelines for such decisions. All parameters on the list are reviewable by the Ministry of Health four times a year. Since these decisions fall outside the Slovak Administrative Code, there is no formal process for the decisions to be appealed by the companies. The new regulation has increased the subjectivity of the Board's decision-making, thereby minimizing the predictability and transparency of the process.

Slovenia

Non-Slovene pharmaceutical companies have expressed concern about the government of Slovenia's non-transparent procedures in pricing and reimbursement. In November 2005, the government moved to implement Therapeutic Reference Pricing (TRP), most likely as an attempt at reducing government expenditures. Pharmaceutical stakeholders have claimed that this penalizes innovation while rewarding imitation. Through proactive measures by innovative companies, TRP was left out of the New Medicine Law. The threat of TRP continues and will continue as the government of Slovenia tries to reduce government spending on health without enacting measures unpopular with citizens.

Innovative U.S. drug manufacturers continue to face pricing issues, with the government setting price limitations based on a "basket" of "European average prices." Currently, the government is considering an option to match its price to the lowest price in the "basket" rather than the average, threatening to further inhibit Slovenian consumers' access to new drugs. Slovenian regulations require health professionals to prescribe drugs with the lowest price in their group as stated on the Interchangeable Drug List (IDL). These are the only drugs that are fully reimbursed under the state insurance plan.

United Kingdom (UK)

The UK's National Institute for Health and Clinical Excellence (NICE) is responsible for judging the clinical and cost-effectiveness of new and existing drugs, treatments, and medical devices, and providing guidance to the UK's National Health Service (NHS) on whether the NHS should fund a treatment. NICE's review is in addition to the normal national approval process through the UK's Medicines and Healthcare Products Regulatory Agency. The slow implementation and lack of transparency of NICE guidance is a disincentive for U.S. and European pharmaceutical companies to launch innovative products in the UK.

The UK also limits the profits pharmaceutical companies are allowed on their sales to NHS through the Pharmaceutical Price Regulation Scheme (PPRS), which requires companies that sold more than $2 million worth of branded medicines to the NHS in the previous year to reduce prices by 7 percent. Companies that exceed the profit target by more than 40 percent must refund the excess either as a lump sum payment to the Department of Health or as price reductions to the NHS. The Office of Fair Trading has recommended replacing the PPRS with a value-based pricing system.

Uranium Imports

The United States is concerned that EU policies may restrict the import into the EU of enriched uranium and possibly downstream goods such as nuclear fuel, nuclear rods, and assemblies. Since 1992, the EU has maintained strict quantitative restrictions on imports of enriched uranium to protect its domestic producers. Since 1994, these restrictions have been applied in accordance with the terms of the Corfu Declaration, a joint European Council and European Commission policy statement that has never been made public or notified to the WTO. The Corfu Declaration appears to impose explicit quotas on imports of enriched uranium, limiting imports to only about 20 percent of the European market. The United States has raised concerns about the import quotas and the non-transparent nature of the Corfu Declaration and its application. Further, the United States is closely monitoring whether future EU agreements with Russia under negotiation in the nuclear area will follow WTO rules on import quotas and transparency.

STANDARDS, TESTING, LABELING, AND CERTIFICATION

Overview

With the decline of traditional transatlantic trade barriers, EU regulatory measures are increasingly viewed as impediments for U.S. exporters of manufactured and agricultural products. Compliance with divergent technical regulations and standards for products sold in the United States and the EU imposes additional costs on U.S. exporters (e.g., duplicative testing, product redesign) and increases the time required to bring a product to market. Such costs for U.S. exporters are compounded by a lack of transparency in the development of EU regulations and a lack of meaningful opportunity for non-EU stakeholders to provide input on draft EU regulations and standards. To address these systemic concerns, the United States continues to promote greater U.S.-EU regulatory cooperation and enhanced transparency in the EU regulatory system.

Despite often sharing similar regulatory objectives, the U.S.-EU dialogue frequently is unable to promptly resolve regulatory-based trade problems. In particular, many U.S. exporters view the EU's growing use of its "precautionary principle" to restrict or prohibit trade in certain products, in the absence of a scientific justification for doing so, as a pretext for market protection. Further, EU regulatory barriers are often compounded by multiple and overlapping measures affecting particular products. Poultry, beef, agricultural biotechnology products, and wine are examples of products that face multiple layers of restrictive regulation in the EU marketplace. To illustrate:

- U.S. efforts to reopen the EU to U.S. poultry exports have been hindered by multiple obstacles. As a result, resolution of any one obstacle (e.g., the EU allowing the use of alternative antimicrobial treatments on poultry meat) would not necessarily result in a reopening of trade due to the existence of other obstacles (such as requirements regarding on-farm practices for raising poultry). Beef trade faces similar problems.

- U.S. exporters of agricultural biotechnology products have been harmed not only by the *de facto* moratorium on approving new products but also by the existence of certain Member State prohibitions on products already approved for marketing within the European Community. This was the subject of a successful WTO challenge by the United States.
- Despite the recent conclusion of a U.S.-EU agreement on wine trade, U.S. wine exporters are still confronted by the uncertainty surrounding the EU's restrictions on labeling practices, as well as high tariffs, heavy subsidization of EU wine producers, uneven recognition of wine labels at the Member State level, failure to provide protection for foreign GIs, and public affairs campaigns denigrating the quality of U.S. wine.

Standardization

Given the massive U.S.-EU trade relationship and the volume of EU standardization work in regulated market segments, European standards activities are of considerable importance to U.S. exporters. A number of standards-related problems continue to impede U.S. exports, including a general inability to participate in the formation of EU standards and occasional reliance on design-based, rather than performance-based, standards. Disparities between the practices of some European conformity assessment bodies add to the frustration and cost for American exporters. In addition, there are concerns related to the procedures, responsibilities (e.g., accountability and redress), and lack of transparency in the Member States, the European Commission, and the European standards bodies. In the case of many sectors, European directives and their relevant standards pose a significant impediment to American exports.

Pressure Equipment
In May 2002, the EU Pressure Equipment Directive (PED) entered into force, imposing new requirements on manufacturers of such equipment. Previously, pressure equipment manufacturers could demonstrate conformity based on standards for material specifications, including the

U.S. ASME Code. Manufacturers using the ASME Code may now be excluded from the EU market because the European standards incorporate material specifications slightly different from those found in the ASME Code. In the absence of a full set of harmonized EU standards, the PED permits manufacturers to file for an EAM (European Approval of Materials); however, few requests for EAMs have been approved so far. Another option, the Particular Material Appraisal (PMA), is a costly process for which there are no clearly defined procedures in the PED. In light of these factors, U.S. manufacturers seek continued acceptance of materials that meet the ASME code that have been widely used in Europe for decades prior to the PED. In an effort to bring the two sides closer together, U.S. and EU officials and stakeholders agreed to a pilot project to eliminate redundant testing requirements for materials. The two sides are beginning technical cooperation, starting with an attempt to harmonize several testing standards.

The Netherlands

The Dutch parliament has shelved consideration of a proposed amendment to the Environmental Management Act that could have significantly impacted U.S. exporters of wood products. The amendment would have required assessment criteria to be equivalent to one particular certification program to the exclusion of others, require a declaration on where the wood is produced, as well as an auditor's report of delivery. The amendment was shelved following an agreement between the Dutch government, wood industry, and NGOs on a certifying system to test sustainable produced wood.

Agricultural Biotechnology Products

Since 1998, the European Union's Council of Ministers has not managed to assemble a qualified majority of EU Member States in support of agricultural biotechnology product approvals, despite the lack of any legitimate health or safety reason not to approve them. While the European Commission granted approval for a limited number of biotechnology products under its legislative authority, the United States considers that the EU continues to lack a predictable, workable process for approving these products in a way that reflects scientific, rather than political factors. At the level of the EU Council, it is clear that many Member States still actively support and maintain a *de facto* moratorium on product approvals.

In May 2003, the United States initiated a WTO dispute settlement process related to the EU's *de facto* moratorium on approvals of biotechnology products and to the existence of individual Member State marketing prohibitions on previously approved biotechnology products. The panel hearing this dispute delivered its interim report in February 2006 and published the final report on September 29. The European Commission has not yet indicated how it plans to implement the panel report.

Several Member States have imposed marketing bans (safeguard measures) on some biotechnology products that had been previously approved at the EU level. On June 24, 2005, the Environment Council rejected, by a qualified majority, the eight Commission proposals to lift safeguard measures imposed by five Member States against biotechnology maize. On October 5, 2005, the European Court of Justice ruled against Upper Austria's effective ban on growing biotechnology crops since there was no scientific evidence to substantiate the ban.

Recent public attacks on the EU's independent scientific authority, the European Food Safety Authority (EFSA), appear to be slowing down the approval process. Specifically, the European Commission published a proposal on April 12 on improving the agriculture biotechnology legislative framework that has been implemented retroactively on EFSA biotechnology food safety opinions. In 2006, the Austrian EU Presidency presided over the debate on EFSA and also attempted to revise decision-making criteria for biotechnology approvals, despite the fact that the Member States had approved the decision-making procedure presently in place. The Environment Council did push the Commission to revisit criteria for EFSA scientific opinions; this could create further undue delays of biotechnology product approvals.

On August 18, 2006, USDA announced that a biotechnology rice variety (LL 601) had been detected in samples taken from U.S. long grain rice. At that time, LL601 was not approved for marketing in either the EU or the United States, but has since been deregulated in the United States. While both the EU and the United States have reviewed the available scientific data and concluded that there are no human health, food safety, or environmental concerns associated with this rice, the DG for Health and Consumer Protection (DG SANCO) directed the 25 Member States to test products for the presence of LL 601 rice in their markets. Trace elements were found in both bulk shipments and in processed food products, resulting in product rejection and destruction. However, differences in testing protocols on both sides of the Atlantic raised questions about the reliability of testing. In response, the U.S. Government began intensive talks with EU officials to establish a common protocol for bulk shipments from the United States in an effort to avoid mandatory testing upon arrival in the EU. These talks failed to produce an agreement and the Commission, with Member State support, introduced mandatory testing at destination, effective October 23, 2006. This has had the effect of continuing the effective embargo on trade in rice from the United States.

Co-Existence

In accordance with the European Commission's guidance document on the co-existence of biotechnology and conventional crops, which recommends a regional approach to co-existence issues, a number of Member States (including Spain, Denmark, Germany, Italy, the Netherlands and most regions in Austria) have drafted new co-existence laws or have chosen to provide industry guidance. While the decrees/laws vary substantially from country to country, they generally require extensive control, monitoring and reporting of biotechnology crops. The European Commission may initiate infringement proceedings against a Member State's co-existence law if it is judged to be incompatible with EU law. However, there is no time limit on how quickly the Commission must act. The European Commission and the Austrian EU Presidency co- hosted a Conference on Co-existence in April 2006. In addition to the Conference's conclusion that there was a need for all Member States to define their co-existence policy, there was a call for a European-wide seed threshold to assist governments in choosing scientifically-based separation distances.

Traceability and Labeling

In April 2004, EC Regulations 1829/2003 and 1830/2003 governing the approval, traceability and labeling of biotechnology food and feed became effective. The regulations include mandatory traceability and labeling for all biotechnology and downstream products. Among the traceability rules are requirements that information that a product contains or consists of biotechnology products must be transmitted to each operator throughout the entire supply chain. Operators must also have a standardized system in place to keep information about biotechnology products and to identify the operator by whom and to whom it was transferred for a period of five years from each transaction. The requirements include an obligation to label appropriate products and to indicate if the food is different from its conventional counterpart in composition, nutritional value, intended use or health implications.

In some cases, these burdensome directives have already severely restricted market access for U.S. food suppliers because food producers have reformulated their products to eliminate the use of biotechnology products. Food producers have indicated concern about needing to find expensive or limited alternatives. The Directives generally are anticipated to have a negative impact on a wide range of U.S. exports, including processed food exports. The European Commission issued a report in spring 2006 on the implementation of the traceability and labeling directive that was largely inconclusive because of the limited number of products containing biotechnology material that have entered the EU market.

Austria

The Austrian Biotechnology Law allows, in principle, for planting of biotechnology crops. However, strict and complicated rules on liability and compensation still represent a *de facto* barrier against all EU-approved biotechnology crops. All nine Austrian provinces have passed biotechnology precautionary bills to protect their organic and small-scale agricultural sector. Three Austrian ordinances still ban the planting of all EU-approved biotechnology crops and a new fourth ordinance bans the marketing of a biotechnology oilseed rape. Under current Austrian rules, unapproved biotechnology events must not be detected in conventional seeds ("zero tolerance"), but EU-approved events may be present in conventional and organic seeds up to 0.1 percent.

Driven by political rather than scientific factors, the government of Austria has effectively banned most agricultural biotechnology applications apart from research. All major Austrian supermarket chains have banned biotechnology products from their shelves, even those labeled according to EC regulations.

Baltic Countries

In Estonia, Latvia, and Lithuania, the scientific community in each country broadly agrees that the technology is safe and can provide benefits to producers and consumers. Some officials in Estonia and Latvia have expressed interest in the potential use of biotechnology for industrial purposes, such as the production of paper from high-starch potatoes and cellulosic biofuel from willows and grasses.

Despite concerns, all three countries are moving forward with developing co-existence regulations and agreed to a general framework for such regulations in July 2006. The proposed documentation and registration requirements for farmers wishing to plant biotechnology seed are quite onerous in each of the country's draft proposals. Currently, interest in biotechnology among Baltic farmers does not seem high, because the region's climate is less favorable for the biotechnology seed varieties currently approved in the EU. New seed varieties could stimulate interest, but onerous co-existence requirements could slow or even stifle use.

Cyprus

Cyprus has adopted increasingly tough standards for biotechnology products, which, in some cases, exceed minimum EU requirements. For example: (a) GOC application requirements for new agricultural biotechnology crops are more arduous than in other EU countries; (b) permits for such crops must be renewed every five years; and (c) the GOC has declared as "GMO-free" areas under the Natura 2000 project (corresponding to 14 percent of Cyprus). Biotechnology products that are already licensed in the EU may circulate in Cyprus freely. However, biotechnology organisms must be approved, even if they are already licensed in other EU countries.

France

A biotechnology bill transposing EU Directives 1998/81 and 2001/18, which provides for coexistence measures, and revises the regulatory approval process for France, passed the

Senate in March 2006 but has not been considered by the National Assembly. It is unlikely that the bill will proceed further in the legislative process before the May 2007 national elections. The French government will be required to pay penalties to the European Commission (EC) if the Directives 1998/91 and 2001/18 are not transposed on time. Notwithstanding the lack of co-existence regulations in France, biotechnology corn production increased from 500 hectares in 2005 to 5,000 hectares in 2006. France has consistently entertained applications for biotechnology research plots and accepted 30 applications for research in open-fields in 2006. In addition, since 2004, France has, at the EU level, voted in favor of certain biotechnology products under Directive 2001/18.

In 2005 and 2006, anti-biotechnology activists destroyed more than 50 percent of test fields in France and recently attacked several commercial biotechnology corn fields. The French Ministry of Agriculture issued two press communiques this summer condemning the destruction of research and commercial crops that are produced legally in France. The communiques were particularly noteworthy, since before these incidents, the Ministry did not have a strong track record of condemning such behavior. Agriculture Minister Bussereau affirmed his support to farmers and researchers stating that firm instructions had been given to local authorities to guarantee the security of biotechnology test plots and that legal proceedings will be launched systematically against those who destroy biotechnology crops.

Germany

In November 2005, the new grand coalition government decided to re-examine the biotechnology law with the goal of making the legal rules for biotechnology crops more practicable. As of November 2006, this had yet to occur because of the lack of consensus on several key points, including liability. Also in November 2005, Germany approved five Bt corn varieties for commercial planting. In 2006, farmers mainly in eastern Germany planted 950 hectares of Bt corn compared to about 300 hectares in 2005. The seed industry is optimistic that the Bt corn area will rise further in 2007. In the summer of 2006, farmers interested in biotechnology seeds founded a self-help organization for farmers interested in biotechnology crop production called InnoPlanta AGIL which has carried out several outreach and educational activities. Despite these positive developments, the number of vandalistic field destructions increased in 2006.

Greece

Greece has opposed the introduction of biotechnology seeds for field tests, despite support for such tests by Greek farmers and Greece's agricultural science community.

Hungary

Extensive biotechnology research is taking place in Hungary, and the Hungarian government has allowed field tests for herbicide resistant corn, wheat and other crops. Although Hungary is required to adopt all relevant EU biotechnology legislation, Hungary has not yet prepared the national application rules for the EU biotechnology regulations on food and feed, and traceability and labeling. In early 2007, the EU Council again upheld Hungary's "safeguard clause" and with it a January 2005 Hungarian moratorium on corn varieties containing the Monsanto MON 810 event. The measure bans the production, use, distribution, and import of hybrids deriving from the MON 810 maize lines. The ban applies to seed producers and distributors as well as farmers. The moratorium is being addressed in the context of the country's co-existence legislation, which is currently awaiting Parliamentary approval and serves as the regulatory framework through which Hungary views biotechnology in the agricultural sector.

Italy

There are varying positions on agricultural biotechnology products among Italy's Ministries of Health, Agriculture, and Environment. The Ministry of Agriculture has imposed rigorous thresholds for seed purity in an effort to minimize the risk of adventitious presence. Current regulations permit only the minimum detectable 0.05 percent of biotechnology seeds to be present. In the case of soybeans used for animal feed, the Ministry of Agriculture allows the use of imported biotechnology beans, as the Ministry is unable to meet Italian feed demand from non-biotechnology sources.

On November 29, 2004, the Regional Administrative Tribunal (TAR) of Lazio (which includes Rome) annulled the decree banning the commercialization of four EU-approved biotechnology corn varieties (BT11, MON 810, MON 809, and T25). Separately, in March 2006, the Italian High Court ruled that coexistence legislation enacted by Parliament was unconstitutional. In its ruling, the Court stated that Italy's regions are responsible for the development of co-existence legislation. The regions are engaged in this task, although only a few are expected to consider the interest of farmers in the process. The United States is concerned that this legislation could discourage biotechnology crop planting and will watch developments closely.

Luxembourg

Luxembourg remains staunchly opposed to biotechnology crops, banning the marketing or growing of biotechnology crops and opposing the approval of new biotechnology products for EU use. Luxembourg acknowledges that their national ban is a problem for the EU with regard to WTO obligations (Luxembourg was one of the six member states whose bans were the subject of a WTO dispute in which the WTO dispute panel found such bans to be inconsistent with WTO rules), but the issue remains politically explosive due to highly vocal opposition. Despite the EU Commission's continued efforts in 2006 to have Luxembourg withdraw its national ban, the law remains in effect. Legislation which would regulate the growing of biotechnology crops in Luxembourg remained stalled in a parliamentary committee for a second year. However, the Luxembourg Chamber of Deputies adopted a law implementing EU directive 98/44/CE on the legal protection of biotechnological inventions of 1998.

Poland

The Polish government opposes the use of biotechnology and in mid-2006 enacted legislation that bans the sale and registration (but not planting) of biotechnology seeds. In two years, it will prohibit the production, import and sale of animal feed produced from transgenic crops.

In contrast to the government's opposition to biotechnology products, many well-respected local scientists and a number of farm groups support their use. Support among farmers is growing along with the spread of the European corn borer into Poland's western corn producing regions.

The EU has notified Polish officials that their seed ban violates EU obligations but the government remains committed to its legislation. The ban may raise WTO concerns, as WTO obligations require that sanitary and phytosanitary regulations be based on science. If the ban on biotechnology feed were to be enforced, it could have a devastating impact on Polish livestock production, especially pork and poultry.

With the exception of some animal feed sales, the United States currently has little biotechnology trade with Poland, but there is strong interest in marketing transgenic seeds in the country. Poland currently does not produce any transgenic crops, with the possible exception of minor quantities grown for research purposes. Poland annually imports about 1.5 to 2.0 MMT of soybean meal, most of which is produced from transgenic soybeans. While the majority of these imports are from Argentina, some are transshipped U.S.-origin soybeans.

Portugal

Portugal, one of only five EU countries to cultivate biotechnology crops, began planting biotechnology corn in 2005. Biotechnology crops are expected to reach 1400 hectares in 2006, twice the 2005 level. However, 2005 co-existence legislation and current proposed legislation to establish biotechnology-free areas will likely constrain further expansion of biotechnology corn.

In early 2006, the government of Portugal established the Authority for Food and Economic Safety (AFES) under the auspices of the Ministry of Economy. AFES works with the European Food Safety Authority to conduct biotechnology assessment, risk monitoring and communications.

Romania

Romania's adoption of EU legislation on biotechnology has resulted in significant change of policy regarding biotechnology. Before 2006, Romania was the largest planter of biotechnology soybeans in Europe. Despite protests from domestic producers, Romania decided to drastically limit biotechnology cultivation in 2006 and to totally ban it in 2007.

Spain

Spain remains the EU member with the largest area under biotechnology corn cultivation. However, the current government tends to take a more restrictive position with respect to agricultural biotechnology. As a result, Spain typically abstains on Commission proposals for approving biotechnology events. Moreover, Spain recently released proposed regulations that would impose 220 meter distance requirements between conventional, organic and biotechnology crops. If approved, biotechnology use is likely to decline in Spain.

Barriers Affecting Trade in Cattle, Beef, Poultry, and Animal by-Products

A variety of EU measures, outlined below, have the effect of severely restricting U.S. exports of livestock products to the European Union market. The adoption of EU non-tariff barriers by Romania and Bulgaria in the process of acceding to the EU in 2006 resulted in the loss of significant markets for U.S. exports.

EU Hormone Directive

In 1988, the EU provisionally banned the use of substances that have a hormonal growth-promoting effect in raising food-producing animals. This action effectively banned the export to the EU of beef from cattle raised in the United States. The use of hormone implants is approved by the U.S. Food and Drug Administration and is a common practice in U.S. beef cattle production. The United States launched a formal WTO dispute settlement procedure in May 1996 challenging the EU ban. In 1999, the WTO ruled that the EU's ban was inconsistent with the WTO Agreement on the Application of Sanitary and Phytosanitary Measures (SPS Agreement) because it was not based on a scientific risk assessment, and authorized the United States to impose sanctions on EU products with an annual trade value of $116.8 million.

In September 2003, the EU announced the entry into force of an amendment (EC Directive 2003/74) to its Hormone Directive (EC Directive 96/22). The new Directive recodified the ban on the use of estradiol for growth promotion purposes and established provisional bans on the five other growth hormones included in the original EU legislation. With enforcement of this new Directive, the EU argued that it was now in compliance with the earlier WTO ruling.

At present, the United States continues to apply 100 percent duties on $116.8 million of U.S. imports from the EU. In November 2004, the EU requested WTO consultations with the United States on this matter, claiming that U.S. sanctions were no longer justified. The dispute is now before a WTO panel, which is expected to publish its findings in the spring of 2007. The United States maintains that the revised EU measure cannot be considered to implement WTO recommendations and rulings related to this matter, and that the U.S. sanctions therefore remain authorized.

Animal by-Products Legislation

In October 2002, the European Commission approved EC Regulation 1774/2002, which regulates the importation of animal by-products not fit for human consumption. The regulation went into force in May 2004. During 2003, intensive technical discussions between U.S. and EU officials successfully addressed some issues and prevented trade disruption for a significant portion (at least $300 million) of U.S. exports to the EU of animal by-products. However, it is estimated that with the publication of the final text, about $100 million of U.S. animal by-product exports to the EU remain adversely affected to some degree. In particular, the United States remains concerned about various outstanding issues for which the EU has not provided risk assessments, such as a ban on the use of dead-in-transport poultry in pet food. The U.S. exports remaining most exposed to this regulation are dry pet food, other animal protein products, and some hides and skins. It is unclear as to the regulation's overall effect on further downstream products such as certain *in vitro* diagnostic products that may use animal by-products. In October 2005, the Commission presented a report to the EU Parliament recommending amendments to EC Regulation 1774/2002. Any agreed amendments would need to be voted on by the EU Parliament. The U.S. commented extensively on this report, which was also notified to the WTO. Furthermore, the Commission organized a conference on animal by-products in Brussels on September 20, 2006, following three sessions of a Training Initiative Pilot Program which took place in June, July and August 2006. The United States used this opportunity to share with Member States the numerous problems exporters have encountered with the 1774/2002 Regulation resulting from inconsistent interpretation and implementation by Member States. The U.S. Government will continue to seek progress on this issue in the short- and mid-term. A series of other products and issues under discussion are not expected to make it through the EU legislative process for another two years.

Poultry Meat Restrictions

U.S. poultry meat exports to the EU have been banned since April 1, 1997, because U.S. poultry producers currently use washes of low-concentration anti-microbial treatments (AMTs) to reduce the level of pathogens in poultry meat production, a practice not permitted by the EU sanitary regime. In December 2005, the European Commission's Food Safety Authority completed studies of four AMTs and found them to be safe, and in February 2006, the European Commission's Health and Consumer Protection Directorate General circulated the first draft of its proposal to allow those substances to be used on poultry meat in the EU market. That draft regulation proposed to ban the use of more than one AMT and require poultry treated with AMTs to be rinsed after treatment. These two requirements are not fully consistent with U.S. production methods and will limit some U.S. exporters' ability to trade poultry to the EU under this regulation, but would nonetheless mark a lifting of the ban on U.S. poultry exports. In 2007, the United States will continue to push for a regulation allowing the use of AMTs to be finalized in the EU legislative process.

Lithuania
Lithuanian veterinary officials have started to more strictly enforce EU transshipment regulations, especially those that they interpret to apply to labeling. As a result, products with labels that do not include the language of the destination country or with labels that indicate a destination other than the actual destination may be detained. For example, Lithuanian officials recently detained a shipment of U.S. poultry with labeling in Chinese destined for Kazakhstan, even though Kazakhstan permits such imports.

Finland and Sweden
The European Commission has granted both Finland and Sweden extensions of the derogations approved in their EU accession agreements, which allow both countries to continue to enforce stricter salmonella controls and stricter border controls for live animals (quarantine) than those enforced by other EU Member States. These countries also impose strict requirements regarding the importation of fresh (including frozen) meat, ground meat, and meat preparations, (with the exception of heat-treated meat) and table eggs.

Romania and Bulgaria
The European Commission has granted some Romanian and Bulgarian domestic meat-processing facilities a transition period for adopting certain EU poultry and pork meat requirements until 2009. Imports from non-EU sources, such as the United States, however, must immediately comply with the EU requirements, creating a national treatment issue. This

change has practically put an end to trade in what was previously the top U.S. agricultural export to Romania, frozen broiler chickens. U.S. pork imports have also been adversely affected. The United States has raised these national treatment concerns in the WTO Sanitary and Phytosanitary Committee.

Barriers Affecting Vitamins and Health Food Products

France: France transposed its list of permitted vitamin and mineral preparations to be added in food supplements as established in EU Directives 2002/46/EC and 2006/37/EC in March 2006. However, France adopted a decree in May 2006 to set tolerance levels and daily allowance for vitamins and minerals that are not in accordance with standards established in relevant EU Directives.

Greece

In implementing the EU Food Supplement Directive, Greece restricted the sale of protein-based meal replacement products to pharmacies and specialized stores, limiting the ability of U.S. companies to sell such products through direct sales.

Spain

Spain has restrictive practices with respect to the use of vitamins and health food products. Since March 2002, Ministry of Health inspectors have raided health food shops and removed 227 different types of health food products from the market. Although the EU passed a new Directive on dietetics, Spain maintains its restrictive policy with regard to limits in vitamin and mineral composition.

EMERGING REGULATORY BARRIERS

In addition to the previously mentioned trade barriers arising from EU policies regarding standards, testing, labeling, and certification, the United States has serious concerns about the ongoing development of new regulations that would appear to have serious adverse consequences for U.S. exporters in the future. The United States is actively engaging the European Union with respect to the issues outlined below.

EU Directive on Wood Packaging Material (WPM)

In February 2005, the EU suspended its plan to implement a new Directive on wood packaging material (WPM) that could affect up to $80 billion worth of U.S. agricultural and commercial exports to the EU that are shipped on wooden pallets or in wood packaging materials. The Directive, published by the European Commission on October 5, 2004, would place a debarking requirement, in addition to heat treatment fumigation, on WPM from the United States and other countries.

The EU Directive is more restrictive than the international standard established by the International Plant Protection Convention (IPPC), Guidelines for Regulating Wood Packaging Material in International Trade (IPSM-15). IPPC members, including the EU, approved ISPM-15 to harmonize and safeguard WPM requirements in world trade. IPPC members approved specific treatments and the marking of WPM but did not support a debarking requirement in the absence of a scientific justification. The IPPC continues to assess emerging scientific studies related to this issue. EU Member States approved a further postponement of the unilateral debarking requirement until December 2008, with a review of the issue scheduled for 2007.

Chemicals

In October 2003, the European Commission presented its proposal for a massive overhaul of existing EU chemicals regulation. The proposal, called REACH (Registration, Evaluation, and Authorization of Chemicals), requires all chemicals produced or imported into the EU in volumes above one ton per year (affecting approximately 30,000 chemicals) to be registered in a central database, and imposes new testing and marketing requirements. Chemicals of very high concern would need an authorization for use in the EU. This legislation could impact virtually every industrial sector, from automobiles to textiles because it regulates substances on their own, in preparations, and in products.

While the United States supports the EU's objectives of protecting human health and the environment, it questions the workability of the present approach. A risk-based approach would allow the EU to address its environmental, public health and safety priorities while avoiding the imposition of disproportionate costs, large burdens on vital substance and product manufacturers and importers, and avoid the likely adverse impacts on trade and innovation. Many of the EU's trading partners expressed similar concerns.

In December 2006, the EU reached agreement on its final regulation. REACH is to enter into force on June 1, 2007. The United States will continue to monitor closely the implementation of this EU regulation and remain engaged constructively with the EU to ensure that U.S. interests are protected.

Cosmetics

The EU's cosmetics directive calls for an EU-wide ban on animal testing within the EU for cosmetic products and an EU-wide ban on the marketing/sale of cosmetic products that have been tested on animals, whether such testing has occurred inside or outside the EU. It will prohibit the sale in the EU of

U.S. cosmetics products tested on animals as of 2009 or 2013 (depending on the type of test) or earlier if the European Community has approved an alternative testing method.

To minimize possible trade disruption, the U.S. Government and the European Commission have embarked on a joint project to develop harmonized, alternative, non-animal testing methods. The project involves cooperation between the U.S. Interagency Coordinating Committee on the Validation of Alternative Methods and the European Center for the Validation of Alternative Methods (ECVAM). The aim is to develop agreed alternative testing methods that would be submitted to the OECD process for international validation. The validation of alternative methods is a long and expensive process, taking an average of seven years. The EC is actively encouraging ECVAM to pursue alternative methods in the near term.

Waste Management (WEEE and RoHS Directives)

In January 2003, the European Union adopted two Directives in an effort to address environmental concerns related to the growing volume of waste electrical and electronic equipment. The Waste Electrical and Electronic Equipment (WEEE) Directive focuses on the collection and recycling of electrical and electronic equipment waste. The Restriction of the Use of certain Hazardous Substances (RoHS) Directive addresses restrictions on the use of certain substances in electrical and electronic equipment, such as lead, mercury, cadmium, and certain flame-retardants.

Under the WEEE Directive, producers are held individually responsible for financing the collection, treatment, and recycling of the waste arising from their new products as of August 2005. Producers have the choice of managing their waste on an individual basis or participating in a collective scheme. Waste from old products is the collective responsibility of existing producers based on their market share.

Member States were required to transpose the WEEE Directive into national law by August 13, 2004, and to implement it by August 13, 2005. Many Member States are behind in their implementation and do not have their national WEEE registration systems in place. The WEEE Directive required that by December 31, 2006, Member States ensure a target of at least four kilograms of electrical and electronic equipment per inhabitant per year is being collected from private households. The policy is intended to create an incentive for companies to design more environment-friendly products.

Under the RoHS Directive, as of July 1, 2006, the placing on the European market of electrical and electronic equipment containing lead, mercury, cadmium, hexavalent chromium, polybrominated biphenyls, and polybrominated diphenyl ethers is prohibited, with some limited exemptions. The Commission Decision, published on August 18, 2005, established maximum concentration values of 0.1 percent by weight in homogenous materials for lead, mercury, hexavalent chromium, polybrominated biphenyls (PBB), and polybrominated diphenyl ethers (PDBE) and 0.01 percent by weight in homogenous materials for cadmium.

Some U.S. companies seeking to comply with the RoHS Directive claim to face significant commercial uncertainties. Firms assert that they lack sufficient, clear, and legally binding guidance from the EU on product scope and, in cases where technically viable alternatives do not exist, businesses face a lengthy, uncertain, and non-transparent exemption process. The European Commission will consider RoHS exemption requests on an ongoing basis, and will be regularly reviewing the need for existing exemptions. Some exporters claim that the uncertainty about RoHS provisions is having an adverse impact on companies as they must make practical design, production, and commercial decisions without adequate information.

Increasing the uncertainty for U.S. manufacturers is the fact that enforcement of RoHS will be managed at the national level. In the absence of a common approach to approval and established EU-wide standards and test methods, a product may be deemed compliant in one country and non-compliant in another.

Given the substantial impacts of RoHS substance bans on international trade, the U.S. Government has urged the European Commission to provide sufficiently detailed, legally binding guidance to give companies seeking to comply with RoHS commercial certainty. The United States has also urged the Commission to make the exemption process more efficient and transparent so that companies can have definitive answers more promptly on whether and how the Directive will apply to their products and to move towards greater harmonization of approaches in the implementation and enforcement of both Directives.

Battery Directive

In 2003, the European Commission proposed a revised version of the 1991 EU Battery Directive. The aim of the new Directive is to collect and recycle all waste batteries and to prevent their incineration and disposal. Producers must finance the collection, treatment, and recycling of waste batteries. On the issue of nickel cadmium (NiCd), the Commission proposes to set high collection targets rather than a ban. The impact assessment carried out by the Commission identifies this approach for dealing with NiCd batteries as the best option from the environment and economic points of view.

In July 2006, the European Parliament and the EU Council of Ministers agreed on a compromise to revise the 1991 Directive on batteries and accumulators. The new directive bans batteries containing cadmium (at levels above 0.002 percent) and mercury (at levels above 0.0005percent) but there are exceptions for emergency and alarms systems, medical equipment and cordless power tools. It also provides for collecting and recycling targets to be reached by 2016 at the latest.

Energy Using Products (EUP)

The EU framework directive promoting eco-design for energy-using products (EUP) entered into force on August 11, 2005, and EU Member States have until August 11, 2007, to transpose it into national law. Through this directive, the EU means to regulate the integration of energy efficiency and other environmental considerations at the design phase of a product. Once in place, design requirements will become legally binding for all products sold in the EU. The legislation commits the European Commission to draw up a working plan for "implementing measures" by July 2007 that will identify products and set specific standards. The directive contains an initial list of products for which technical studies are now underway, including lighting, office equipment, heating equipment, domestic appliances, air conditioning, and consumer electronics, and energy losses from standby modes. The directive sets out CE marking requirements for the items covered by implementing measures. Industry is most concerned about the possible need for a complete product life cycle analysis, and fears adverse impacts on design flexibility, new product development and introduction, as well as increased administrative burdens.

Metric Directive

Beginning January 1, 2010, the European Union Council Directive 80/181/EEC (Metric Directive) will allow the use of only metric units, and prohibit the use of any other measurements for most products sold in the EU. Going well beyond labeling, the Metric Directive will make the sole use of metric units obligatory in all aspects of life in the European Union, including on labels, packaging, advertising, catalogs, technical manuals, and user instructions. This prohibition will end a longstanding practice in the European trade community of allowing manufacturers flexibility on labeling products. When implemented, the Directive will also create an inconsistency with U.S. law. Unless the Metric Directive implementation date is extended again, as of January 1, 2010, displaying U.S. customary units on a box or label will be illegal in the EU. Most American and European companies which make consumer products will be forced to create separate labels, one for the U.S. market including both metric and imperial measurements, and another for the EU market displaying only metric units, therefore imposing additional costs.

Acceleration of the Phase-Outs of Ozone-Depleting Substances and Greenhouse Gases

As part of a wider climate change program to reduce emissions of greenhouse gases to meet its Kyoto Protocol objectives, the European Union adopted legislation in May 2006 to regulate the emission of fluorinated gases (f-gases). The measures improve the containment of f-gases and introduce specific restrictions on their marketing and use in specific applications. Two pieces of legislation were adopted – a regulation on f-gases used in stationary applications and the other, a Directive regulating hydrofluorocarbons (HFCs) in vehicle air conditioning. The first measure (the "stationary" Regulation) will impact U.S. manufacturers of stationary air conditioning and refrigeration equipment and the companies that produce the chemicals used in them. The second will affect U.S. car and parts manufacturers by phasing-out HFC134a in vehicle air conditioning beginning in 2011 with a complete ban by 2017.

The "stationary" Regulation seeks to improve containment of f-gases by setting minimum standards for inspection and recovery, and, where containment is not feasible, proposes to ban marketing and use of certain applications. Examples of applications using f-gases the Regulation seeks to ban include vehicle tires, non-refillable containers, windows, footwear, one-component foams, self-chilling drinking cans, novelty aerosols and fire extinguishers. The Regulation allows Member States to maintain or introduce stricter protective measures in order to reach Kyoto targets by December 21, 2012. The United States will continue to closely monitor Member States' implementation.

Other Member State Measures

Some EU Member States have their own national practices regarding standards, testing, labeling, and certification. A brief discussion of the additional national practices of concern to the United States follows:

Austria
Austria became the second EU country after Denmark to ban a range of uses of the three fluorinated gases controlled under the Kyoto protocol on climate change. An ordinance that took effect on November 22, 2002, prohibits the use in new sprays, solvents, and fire extinguishers of hydrofluorocarbons (HFCs), perfluorocarbons, and sulphur hexafluoride. The ordinance phases out their use in foams between mid-2003 and the end of 2007. It bans their use in new refrigeration and air-conditioning equipment by the end of 2007. The ban appears to exempt production of HFCs in Austria for the export market. Even under the new EU regulation that focuses on containment instead of bans, the government of Austria has indicated it will try to retain its own national HFC bans.

Denmark
As of January 1, 2007, Danish law bans equipment with charges of less than 150 grams and equipment with charges over 10 kilos. Industry believes these laws will have an adverse effect on the market by creating an additional and disproportionate barrier to products that are manufactured in and distributed across the EU.

Finland
A ban on the importation and sale of new appliances containing hydrochlorofluorocarbons (HCFCs) was imposed on January 1, 2000, and remains in place. The importation of the chemical HCFC is allowed when used for maintenance of old refrigeration appliances using HCFC. New HCFC compounds used for maintenance of refrigeration equipment will be banned as of 2010 and use of all HCFC compounds, including recycled compounds, will be banned as of 2015.

Greece
Greece has not approved the use of corrugated stainless steel pipe (CSST) for use in internal gas industry applications. One U.S. company has been seeking approval to sell in the Greek market since 1997. In late 2005 the Greek standards organization, ELOT, was charged via presidential decree with developing standards for materials used in internal gas installations, which would cover CSST. As of this writing, ELOT has not yet taken the first step of forming a committee that would draft these standards.

GOVERNMENT PROCUREMENT

Since the European Communities is party to the WTO Agreement on Government Procurement (GPA), all of the Member States are also subject to the GPA. This includes Romania and Bulgaria, which became subject to the GPA upon their accession to the EU in January 2007.

In an effort to open government procurement markets within the Member States, the EU in 2004 adopted a revised Utilities Directive (2004/17), covering purchases in the water, transportation, energy, and postal services sectors. Member States were mandated to implement the new Utilities Directive by the end of January 2006, but some EU Member States still had not implemented it.

This Directive requires open, objective bidding procedures but still discriminates against bids with less than 50 percent EU content that are not covered by an international or reciprocal bilateral agreement. The EU-content requirement applies to U.S suppliers of goods and services in the following sectors: water (production, transport, and distribution of drinking water), energy (gas and heat), urban transport (urban railway, automated systems, tramway, bus, trolley bus, and cable), and postal services.

The Directive's discriminatory provisions were waived for heavy electrical equipment manufactured in the United States under the May 1995 Memorandum of Understanding on Government Procurement between the United States and the EU. In 1993, the United States imposed sanctions on a number of Member States for their implementation of discriminatory provisions of an earlier version of the Directive applicable to telecommunications equipment. Directive 2004/17 clarified that those discriminatory provisions no longer applied to the EU telecommunications sector; the United States thus lifted the sanctions (and the EU lifted reciprocal sanctions against U.S. suppliers) on March 1, 2006.

While U.S. suppliers participate significantly in EU government procurement, the lack of availability of statistics on procurements conducted in EU member states makes it difficult to accurately assess the opportunities available under the GPA to U.S. suppliers.

Other Member State Measures

Member States have their own national practices regarding government procurement. Some Member States require offsets in defense procurement, defined as a contract condition or undertaking that encourages local development or improves a party's balance-of-payments accounts, such as the use of domestic content, the licensing of technology, investment, counter-trade, and similar actions or requirements. Defense procurement related to national security is not covered by the GPA and therefore is not subject to GPA standards. A brief discussion of some of the national practices of particular concern to the United States follows.

Austria
U.S. firms continue to report a strong pro-EU bias and pro-Austrian bias in government contract awards. In major defense purchases related to national security, most government procurement regulations do not apply, and offset requirements can reach up to 200 percent of the value of the contract. Defense offsets in Austria are linked to political considerations and transparency remains limited. Austria's largest military procurement to date, the $2 billion purchase of fighter jets in 2002, was awarded in manner that concerned U.S. defense contractors for its lack of transparency, and apparent bias against a U.S. proposal.

Czech Republic
U.S. and other foreign companies express great concern about the transparency of the public procurement process. Many U.S. bidders report that Czech (or other European) bidders

are favored and usually win contract awards despite having less competitive bids and questionable ability to deliver on the terms of the tender. This has been a problem particularly in construction and the purchase of military equipment as well as in the sale of state-owned industries. Parliament passed a new law on government procurement in 2006, but did little to improve procurement transparency. In fact, the law reduces transparency on construction projects by raising the monetary threshold that would mandate an open public tender from 2 million crowns to 6 million crowns. According to Transparency International, only 27 percent of all public tenders were open to multiple bids in 2005. Bribery in government procurement continues to be a problem. A recent World Bank study noted that the Czech Republic is the only country among the ten EU Members that joined the EU in 2004 where the level of corruption worsened since 2003.

France

France has a strong and extremely competitive aerospace and defense manufacturing base. Having allowed only limited privatization in the sector, the French government continues to maintain shares in several major prime contractors. The French defense market remains difficult but not impossible for non-European competition. Even in the case of European competition, French companies are often selected as prime contractors. Nevertheless, U.S. firms do enjoy success as component and systems suppliers in instances where U.S. products provide capabilities required for interoperability, or where the cost of internal development is prohibitive. The Defense Ministry, which handles around 70 percent of the equipment budget, has a tendency to select non-American contractors, even when their bids cost more and take longer to fulfill the contract. These factors have made it difficult for U.S. defense firms to take part in French/European programs.

Greece

Greece imposes onerous qualification requirements on companies seeking to bid on public procurement tenders. Companies must submit documentation from competent authorities indicating that they have paid taxes, are not in or have not been in bankruptcy, have paid in full their social security obligations for their employees, and other requirements. All board members and the managing director must submit certifications from competent authorities that they have not engaged in fraud, money laundering, criminal activity, or similar activities. These requirements are especially difficult for U.S. firms because there are no competent authorities that issue these types of certifications in the United States. In such cases, companies submitting bids are allowed to submit sworn, notarized, and translated statements from corporate officers. Nonetheless, there exists much confusion among Greek authorities as to how U.S. firms may comply with these requirements.

The government of Greece maintains that it is in the process of reforming and simplifying its procurement laws. According to government officials, new legislation will be released within the next several months.

Greece continues to require offsets as a condition for the awarding of defense contracts.

Ireland

Government procurement in Ireland is generally tendered under open and transparent procurement regulations. U.S. companies have raised concerns, however, that they have been successful in only a few national and regional government tenders, particularly for infrastructure-related procurements. U.S. firms complain that lengthy budgetary decisions delay procurements and that unsuccessful bidders often have difficulty obtaining information on the basis for behind the tender award. Once awarded a contract, companies can experience significant delays in finalizing contracts and commencing work. Successful bidders have also subsequently found that tender documentation does not accurately describe the project conditions under which the procurement is to be conducted.

Italy

Procurement authority is widely dispersed with over 22,000 contracting agencies at the national, regional, and local levels (including regions, municipalities, hospitals, universities, etc.). Italy's public procurement sector is noted for its lack of transparency and corruption, which have created obstacles for some U.S. firms.

Since new laws were implemented in the mid-1990s, corruption has been reduced, but not entirely eliminated, especially at the local level. These laws were enacted after corruption scandals, largely associated with irregularities in public works and public procurement of goods and services, caused an overhaul of procurement personnel.

Lithuania

The public procurement process in Lithuania is not always transparent. Complaints persist that some tenders are so narrowly defined that they appear to be drafted so that only one company can provide the good or service. Since 2003, the government of Lithuania (GOL) has required offset agreements as a condition for the award of contracts for procurement of military equipment exceeding LTL 5 million (about $1.8 million). The GOL purchases most U.S. military equipment using U.S. government grant money, which precludes offsets. The GOL has requested offsets for defense purchases it has made using its own funds. This offset requirement adds an unnecessary level of complexity to exporting military equipment to Lithuania.

Portugal

U.S. firms face stiff competition when bidding against EU firms on procurement projects in Portugal. The Portuguese tend to favor EU firms even when bids from U.S. firms appear technically superior or lower in price. There is a general lack of transparency in procurement procedures. It appears to U.S. firms that they are more successful when investing in joint venture projects with Portuguese or other EU firms.

Slovenia

The Slovenian government has said that it intends to improve the transparency of its public procurement process. The Ministry for Public Administration has also said it will create an e-procurement system, but efforts in this area have stalled. American firms continue to express concerns that the public procurement process in Slovenia is non-transparent. Many American bidders report that European firms are favored and usually win contracts in spite of more costly offers and questionable ability to deliver and service their products. This is a problem across the entire range of public procurement, but it seems most prevalent in telecommunications, medical equipment, and defense procurement.

United Kingdom (UK)

The UK defense market is increasingly defined by the terms of the December 2005 Defence Industrial Strategy (DIS). The document highlights specific sectors and capabilities that the government believes are necessary to retain in the UK; in these areas, procurement will generally be based on partnerships between the Ministry of Defence (MoD) and selected companies. One example is the partnership between the MoD and AgustaWestland for rotorcraft procurement. DIS does not preclude partnerships with non-UK companies and U.S. companies with UK operations could be invited by MoD to form partnerships in key programs in the future. Outside of those areas of partnership highlighted in the DIS, defense procurement is to a large extent an open and competitive process. There have, however, been examples of non-competitive procurements in recent years, as well as instances where a U.S. supplier was initially selected, but the decision was subsequently overturned and the contract awarded to a domestic supplier.

SUBSIDIES POLICIES

Government Support for Airbus

Over many years, the governments of France, Germany, Spain, and the United Kingdom have provided subsidies to their respective Airbus member companies to aid in the development, production and marketing of Airbus large civil aircraft. These governments have financed between 33 and 100 percent of the development costs for all Airbus aircraft models ("launch aid") and provided other forms of support, including equity infusions, debt forgiveness, debt rollovers, and marketing assistance, including political and economic pressure on purchasing governments. The EU's aeronautics research programs are driven significantly by a policy intended to enhance the international competitiveness of the European civil aeronautics industry. EU governments have spent hundreds of millions of euros to create infrastructure needed for Airbus programs, including 751 million euros from the City of Hamburg to purchase land that Airbus is using for the Airbus A380 "superjumbo" project and 182 million euros from French authorities to create the AeroConstellation site, which contains the Airbus facilities for the A380. With more than $6 billion in subsidies, the Airbus A380 is the most heavily subsidized aircraft in history. Some EU governments have also made legally binding commitments of launch aid for the new Airbus A350 aircraft, even though Airbus has not yet repaid any of the financing it received for the A380.

The Airbus Integrated Company – successor to the original Airbus consortium and owned by the European Aeronautic, Defense, and Space Company (EADS) – is now the second-largest aerospace company in the world. With more than half of worldwide deliveries of new large civil aircraft over the last few years, Airbus is a mature company that should face the same commercial risks as its global competitors.

In October 2004, following unsuccessful U.S.-initiated efforts to negotiate a new U.S.-EU agreement that would end subsidies for the development and production of large civil aircraft, the United States submitted a WTO consultation request with respect to the launch aid and other forms of subsidies that EU governments have provided to Airbus. Concurrent with the U.S. WTO consultation request, the United States also exercised its right to terminate the 1992 U.S.–EU bilateral agreement on large civil aircraft. The consultations failed to resolve the U.S. concerns, however, and a renewed effort to negotiate a solution ended without success in April 2005.

Therefore, on May 31, 2005, the United States submitted a WTO panel request. The WTO established the panel on July 20, 2005, and panel proceedings are currently ongoing. U.S. officials have consistently noted their willingness to negotiate a new bilateral agreement on large civil aircraft, even while the WTO litigation proceeds, but have insisted that any such agreement must end launch aid and other direct subsidies for the development and production of such aircraft.

Government Support for Airbus Suppliers

Belgium

The federal government of Belgium, in coordination with Belgium's three regional governments, subsidizes Belgian aircraft component manufacturers that supply parts to the Airbus Integrated Company. Industry sources report about 160 million euros remain from a 195 million federal-regional subsidy package for Airbus A380-related research and development that started in 2001, and that costs covered to date have netted orders worth 1.3 billion euros for the A380. Belgium claims the program was structured in accordance with the 1992 bilateral agreement and covers non-recurring costs. On October 14, 2005, the Belgian federal government made a decision in principle to assist Belgian aviation part producers with 150 million euros of reimbursable public financing, available for nonrecurring development costs for the Airbus A350. Airbus's redesign of the A350 has delayed implementation of this program.

France

In addition to the launch aid that the French government provided for the development of the Airbus A380 super-jumbo aircraft in 2005, France continues to provide reimbursable advances for Airbus programs, engines, helicopters, and on-board equipment. Appropriations in 2006 totaled 218 million euros, of which 168 million euros are committed to the A380. Overall 2006 appropriations, including 55 million euros in support of research and development by industrialists in the sector, amount to 273 million euros.

Spain

The recently completed Puerto Real factory in Spain's Andalucia region is responsible for constructing 10 percent of Airbus' A380 aircraft. Spain's Ministry of Science and Technology currently subsidizes A380 construction through its agreement to provide 376 million euros in direct assistance through 2013.

Furthermore, the regional government of Andalucia has channeled an additional 13 million euros of State General Administration regional incentive funds and 17.5 million euros of its own funds to subsidize the A380 project. Spain has provided numerous additional grants to Airbus' parent company, EADS.

Government Support for Aircraft Engines

United Kingdom (UK)
In February 2001, the UK government announced its intention to provide up to 250 million pounds to Rolls-Royce to support development of two additional engine models for large civil aircraft, the Trent 600 and 900.

The UK government characterized this engine development aid as an "investment" that would provide a "real rate of return" from future sales of the engines.

The European Commission announced its approval of a 250 million pounds "reimbursable advance" without opening a formal investigation into whether the advance constituted an illegal (under EU law) state aid. According to a European Commission statement, the "advance will be reimbursed by Rolls-Royce to the UK government in case of success of the program, based on a levy on engine deliveries and maintenance and support activity." Detailed terms of the approved launch aid were not made public. To date, none of the launch aid for the Trent 600 and 900 has been repaid.

Continuing UK government support of Rolls-Royce raises serious concerns about UK and EU adherence to the WTO Subsidies and Countervailing Measures Agreement. U.S. engine suppliers have lost sales of engines and claim that they have encountered suppressed prices in the United States and world markets.

France
The French government-owned engine manufacturer SNECMA merged with technology and communications firm Sagem to form Safran. The government supports the Safran SaM146 propulsive engine program with a reimbursable advance of 140 million euros.

Canned Fruit Subsidies

The EU continues to subsidize shipments of canned peaches as well as the production of apples, prunes, grapes, wine, cherries, and citrus. Although a 1985 U.S.-EU Canned Fruit Agreement brought some discipline to processing subsidies, significant fraud and abuse have undermined the discipline imposed by the Agreement. Growers and producers of peaches receive a range of assistance from producer aid, market withdrawal subsidies, sugar export rebates, producer organization aid, and regional development assistance. The United States will continue to monitor EU subsidies to this sector and evaluate their trade-distorting effects.

Wood Industry Subsidies

Several EU Member States and regional governments within them provided state aid to pulp, paper, and wood processing projects. Germany, in particular, has given aid in the form of grants, loans, and loan guarantees for pulp and paper and wood processing operations, especially in eastern Germany. These subsidy programs are part of the overall combined EU/national regional support programs. This has added substantial new capacity and has contributed to a substantial drop in U.S. pulp and paper exports to the EU and world markets, while fostering a rise in European paper and lumber and wooden panel exports to the United

States and third country markets. A combination of factors, namely robust growth in the construction sector and duties put on Canadian softwood lumber, has also increased the competitiveness of German construction lumber in the United States.

INTELLECTUAL PROPERTY RIGHTS (IPR) PROTECTION

Overview

The EU and its Member States support strong protection for intellectual property rights (IPR). Together, the U.S. and the EU have committed to enforcing IPR in third countries and at our borders in the EU-U.S. Action Strategy endorsed at the June 2006 U.S.-EU Summit. In 2006, the European Commission issued communications on strengthening the criminal law framework to combat intellectual property offenses, and a renewed effort to introduce a community patent.

The United States has raised concerns regarding the IPR practices of the EU or its Member States, either through the U.S. Special 301 process or through WTO Dispute Settlement procedures concerning failure to fully implement the WTO Agreement on Trade-Related Aspects of Intellectual Property Rights (TRIPS). The United States continues to be engaged with the EU and individual Member States on these matters.

In April 2004, the EU adopted a Directive on the enforcement of intellectual and industrial property rights, such as copyright and related rights, trademarks, designs, and patents. This Directive requires all Member States to apply effective and proportionate remedies and penalties that form a deterrent against those engaged in counterfeiting and piracy. Member States are required to have a similar set of measures, procedures, and remedies available for rights holders to defend their IPR. Member States were supposed to have implemented the Directive by April 2006. At present, only about one half of the Member States have transposed the legislation.

Designs

The EU adopted a Regulation introducing a single Community system for the protection of designs in December 2001. The Regulation provides for two types of design protection, directly applicable in each EU Member State: the registered Community design and the unregistered Community design. Under the registered Community design system, holders of eligible designs can use an inexpensive procedure to register designs with the EU's Office for Harmonization in the Internal Market (OHIM). The holders will then be granted exclusive rights to use the designs anywhere in the EU for up to 25 years. Unregistered Community designs that meet the Regulation's requirements are automatically protected for three years from the date of disclosure of the design to the public. Protection for any registered Community design was automatically extended to the ten new EU Member States on May 1, 2004.

The European Commission has proposed amending the Legal Protection of Designs Directive (98/71) by removing Member States' option to maintain design protection for "visible" replacement vehicle parts, such as hoods, bumpers, doors, lamps, rear protection panels, windscreens, and wings. The proposal would allow independent part manufacturers, not linked to the producers of finished vehicles, to compete throughout the EU market for visible replacement parts. Neither non-visible parts, like engine or mechanical parts, nor components in new vehicles would be affected by the proposal.

Patents

Patent filing and maintenance fees in the EU and its Member States are significantly higher than in other countries. Fees associated with the filing, issuance, and maintenance of a patent over its life far exceed those in the United States.

In some countries, such as Portugal, copies of medicines that are still under patent are allowed on the market by the Ministries of Health.

Data Exclusivity

In some of the new Member States in particular, there is a lack of protection for data submitted to obtain marketing approval for pharmaceutical and agricultural chemical products. Article 39.3 of the Trade-Related Aspects of Intellectual Property Rights (TRIPS) Agreement requires such protection.

Bulgaria
The U.S. pharmaceutical industry is concerned about Bulgarian legislation that requires a valid patent as a prerequisite for obtaining data protection. Bulgaria is reportedly considering legislation to eliminate this requirement.

Hungary
Hungary's 2001 ministerial decree on the protection of test data took effect on January 1, 2003. Retroactive protection exists for pharmaceutical products that received first marketing authorization in the EU or Hungary on or after April 12, 2001. However, Hungary generally does not provide an effective system to prevent the issuance of marketing approvals for unauthorized patent-infringing copies of pharmaceutical products, and patent infringements are dealt with by administrative courts lacking expert knowledge, or the power to take injunctive measures.

Poland
Concerns remain over delays in full implementation of the EU data protection regime. Polish law currently supports the EU data protection regime for drugs centrally registered at the EU level. For drugs nationally registered in Poland, however, (in practice, those drugs registered before Poland's EU accession) Polish law provides for only 6 years of data exclusivity. Poland requested that the European Commission delay implementation of the EU requirement for 15 years. The Commission has not informed Poland of its final decision. In addition, while the government has signaled that it is considering implementation of a

coordination mechanism between the Health Ministry and the patent agency, no concrete actions have been taken to do so.

Portugal

In September 2006, Portugal enacted the Consumption of Medicine in Hospitals statute, an adaptation of EU Directive 2004/27/EC. The statute extends data exclusivity from six years to ten and only requires companies to renew licenses once after five years as opposed to every five years. However, the statute also states that the Ministry of Health does not need to cross-check with the Ministry of Economy for existing patents before granting licenses to generic drug manufacturers. According to industry sources, this latter aspect of the legislation may cost U.S. pharmaceutical companies over $500,000 in lost sales and tens of thousands more in legal fees.

Patenting of Biotechnological Inventions

A 1998 EU Directive (98/44) on the legal protection of biotechnological inventions harmonizes EU Member State rules on patent protection for biotechnological inventions. Although Member States were required to bring their national laws into compliance with the Directive by July 2000, some had not yet fully met that obligation, and the European Commission has started legal proceedings at the European Court of Justice against them.

Trademarks

Registration of trademarks with the European Union's Office for Harmonization in the Internal Market (OHIM) began in 1996. OHIM issues a single Community trademark that is valid in all EU Member States.

Madrid Protocol

On October 1, 2004, the European Community acceded to the World Intellectual Property Organization (WIPO) Madrid Protocol, establishing a link between the Madrid Protocol system, administered by WIPO, and the Community Trademark system, administered by OHIM. Community Trademark applicants and holders now are allowed to apply for international protection of their trademarks through the filing of an international application under the Madrid Protocol.

Conversely, holders of international registrations under the Madrid Protocol will be entitled to apply for protection of their trademarks under the Community Trademark system.

Geographical Indications (GI)

The United States has long had concerns that the EU's system for the protection of geographical indications, reflected in Community Regulation 1493/99 for wines and spirits and in previous Regulation 2081/92 for certain other agricultural products and foodstuffs, appears to fall short of what is required under the TRIPS Agreement.

As a result of a WTO dispute launched by the United States, the WTO Dispite Settlement Body ruled on April 20, 2005, that the EC's regulation on food-related geographical indications (GIs) was inconsistent with the EC's obligations under the TRIPS Agreement and the GATT 1994. In its report, the DSB agreed that the EC's GI regulation impermissibly discriminated against non-EC products and persons, and agreed with the United States that the regulation could not create broad exceptions to trademark rights guaranteed by the TRIPS Agreement. In response, the EC published an amended GI regulation in April 2006 that is intended to implement the DSB's recommendations and rulings. The United States continues to have some concerns about this amended regulation and is carefully monitoring its application.

Additional Member State Practices

Belgium

While Belgium transposed the EU Copyright Directive into national law in May 2005, it failed to meet the April 2006 deadline to implement the Enforcement Directive. Belgium also has not implemented EU Regulation 1383/2003 concerning customs actions against goods suspected of infringing certain intellectual property rights. Domestically pirated and parallel-imported DVDs are a growing problem in Belgium. An industry trade association estimates that 250,000 illegal downloads of DVDs occur daily in Belgium, and illegal copies on VHS, CD-R and DVD-R media are distributed by specialty stores, retail outlets, and local and international Internet sites. The recording industry estimates that 85 percent of blank digital media sold in Belgium are used for illegal downloads of music or videos. Annual losses to the U.S. motion picture industry through IPR piracy in Belgium are estimated at over 15 million euros. Belgium's 1994 Copyright Law provides deterrent penalties for piracy, but legal procedures are cumbersome and the court system is overburdened. Obtaining a judicial restraining order against Internet piracy, for example, takes two to three months, and judges demand proof of damages to assign more than token fines. However, the country's first-ever prison sentence for copyright piracy was imposed in April 2006, and Belgium was the first of the EU-15 to ratify the WIPO Copyright Treaty in May 2006.

Bulgaria

Overall optical disc piracy has dropped, but largely due to an increase in piracy over the Internet. While the government has taken a number of significant steps to combat piracy, these actions have not yet led to significant convictions, and the piracy rate has not fallen drastically. Furthermore, Bulgaria is still widely used for the transshipment of pirated compact discs from Russia and Ukraine to the Balkans, Greece, and Turkey. Bulgarian legislation was further amended to harmonize with EU requirements and to provide a better legal framework for efficient IPR enforcement. The laws that were amended include the Law on Copyright and Related Rights, the Law on Patents, the Law on Marks and Geographical Indications, the Law on Industrial Design and Art, 172a (copyright and related rights criminal offences) and 172b (industrial property rights criminal offences) of the Penal Code of the Republic of Bulgaria. In September 2005, the parliament approved the long awaited Law on

Administrative Control over the Manufacture and Distribution of Optical Disc Media, which now requires source identification code on blank optical discs produced in Bulgaria and strengthens the import/export regime for raw materials and equipment involved in optical disk production.

Cyprus

IPR legislation in Cyprus is, on the whole, modern and comprehensive, although enforcement should be further improved. Cyprus has harmonized its IPR regime with EU requirements as part of its accession to the EU in 2004. According to industry sources, the level of DVD and CD piracy continues at roughly 50 percent. Software piracy, largely fueled by small personal computer assembly and sale operations, has declined to 53 percent but is still significantly above the European average. Internet piracy is a growing concern.

Czech Republic

Although the Czech Republic has made progress in strengthening anti-piracy legislation and enforcement, significant problems remain with piracy and counterfeiting in open-air markets near the Czech border. New amendments were added in 2006 to the Copyright Law and the Law on Consumer Protection, which grants the Customs Office, a law enforcement agency with over 6,000 armed inspectors, greater authority to seize counterfeit products and requires all marketplace sellers to register with the municipality. The level of IPR piracy is rising and several IPR watchdog groups, especially from the recording and manufacturing industries, have recommended the Czech Republic be placed on the Special 301 Priority Watch List. There are also problems in court proceedings. Court cases, including IPR related cases, can often stretch to five years on average, and even then the current system for the calculation and collection of damages favor defendants according to legal experts who work in the field.

France

Although the French government has significantly stepped up its efforts to fight piracy, video piracy and unauthorized parallel imports continue to impose losses on U.S. industry, and cable piracy and Internet piracy continue to present further problems in this area. France was the last Member State to pass legislation implementing the EU Copyright Directive in August 2006. Some U.S. stakeholders have expressed concerns with the provisions of that law related to digital rights management and technological protection measures, which may result in the forced disclosure and use of technical information that may be protected by intellectual property such as copyright, patents and trade secrets.

Germany

Non-retail outlets (Internet, print media, mail order, open-air markets) are the primary distribution channels for pirated goods in Germany. Pirated videos, VCDs, and DVDs are sold primarily by residential mail-order dealers who offer the products via the Internet or through newspaper advertisements, or directly sell them in flea markets. German copyright legislation allows the making of private copies, which, although it does not include sharing or downloading of music, has been sometimes misunderstood as being a broad exception. Starting in 2005, the German entertainment industry has blanketed the country with commercials as an information campaign to educate the public regarding the problem of piracy, especially on the Internet. While German federal authorities have been receptive to U.S. IPR concerns, there have been mixed results at the German state-level, which can have broad impact due to Germany's decentralized law enforcement structure. German authorities in several cases have prosecuted pirates who downloaded music and videos from the Internet and then distributed burned CDs or DVDs. In October 2004, they arrested four individuals who ran a major ring selling pirated videos on the Internet. The German government in July 2003 enacted amendments to the German Copyright Act intended to bring it in line with the EU Copyright/"Information Society" Directive. The Ministry of Justice has introduced additional amendments to the copyright law that are likely to be considered by Parliament in 2007. U.S. publishers have expressed a concern that these amendments might result in insufficient protections for copyrighted works, particularly those in digital format. The United States continues to engage the German government on the issue.

Greece

Although protection of intellectual property rights in Greece is better than it was during the last decade, there are troubling signs that violations, particularly in copyrighted audio-visual products and apparel and footwear, are once again on the rise. Despite the existence of adequate IPR legislation, a major problem appears to be a reluctance on the part of Greek judges to sentence IPR violators to jail, or impose fines of a high enough level to act as a deterrent. The United States welcomes initiatives by the government of Greece to make efforts to educate the judiciary on IPR matters to discourage this trend.

Hungary

Hungary acceded to the European Patent Convention on January 1, 2003 and has amended the Hungarian Patent Act accordingly. Act CII of 2003 modified the Hungarian Copyright Act and the Hungarian Design Act in order to bring them in line with the relevant EU legislation. The Hungarian Patent Office implemented the EU Copyright/"Information Society" Directive. In October 2004, Hungary implemented Council Regulation 1383/2003, concerning customs action against goods suspected of infringing certain intellectual property rights. Further, a government decree established a customs task force to accept claims from producers whose trademarks or copyrights were infringed.

Italy

Italy's anti-piracy laws, which also address Internet piracy, are among the toughest in Europe. However, Italy possesses one of the highest overall piracy rates in Western Europe due to a lack of adequate enforcement efforts. Italian judges rarely hand down meaningful jail sentences for cases of IPR theft, and are seen as the weak link in Italy's efforts to combat piracy effectively. Leaders in industry, government and academia all say a change in public perception of the seriousness of IPR crimes is needed before there can be better IPR protection in Italy.

In April 2005, the Italian government created a "High Commissioner" position to coordinate IPR protection. Seizures of counterfeit and pirated goods by Italian authorities increased in the past year, though enforcement varies widely from region to region. Italian law allows police to impose a fine of up to 10,000 euros for possession of fake goods. While this tough measure increased public awareness of IPR crime, there is only sporadic enforcement. Street vendors continue to openly sell pirated and counterfeited goods.

Lithuania

Estimates of piracy levels of optical media, software, and motion pictures in Lithuania vary, but it remains a problem. The situation appears to be improving, however. Lithuania adopted legislation in 2006 that harmonizes Lithuania's laws with EU regulations, strengthening IPR protection by increasing penalties and making it easier for prosecutors to present necessary evidence. The Lithuanian government has demonstrated the political will to enforce IPR protections in specific cases, but the government needs to continue to improve its efficacy in combating piracy. The Lithuanian government made progress in early 2007 by closing down a notorious Internet pirate website, but should continue enforcement efforts agains Internet piracy.

Poland

Poland has shown progress on several elements of IP protection. The Polish government has increased anti-piracy efforts, improving enforcement at the Warsaw Stadium and in the border bazaars frequented by German tourists and others. In addition, the Interministerial Antipiracy Group published an IPR strategy that emphasizes cooperation with industry. Although Poland has made some progress in strengthening border enforcement in conjunction with rights-holders, problems remain both along the eastern and western borders with importation and sale of counterfeit alcohol, tobacco, and pirate optical discs. As border enforcement continues to strengthen, Internet piracy of movies and music is also becoming a more serious problem. According to an anti-piracy group, the Polish court system is currently overburdened with nearly five thousand pending IPR protection cases, many of which are not scheduled to be prosecuted for several years.

Romania

Although authorities have made gradual improvements, the rates of copyright piracy are high in Romania. Levels of DVD piracy have risen to 80 percent, while levels of videocassette piracy are down to 20 percent and the most blatant retail piracy has been eliminated. While product was mainly smuggled into the market in the past, concerns are rising that capacity to produce in Romania may be growing. Another area of concern is the illegal sale of counterfeit decoder devices and stealing video signals from cable services. The appointment in 2003 of a special IPR prosecutor in the General Prosecutor's Office (GPO) and the establishment of a small IPR office in the GPO in 2005 have improved enforcement, but few IPR cases are prosecuted.

Spain

Copyright infringement remains a serious problem with illegal Internet downloads becoming increasingly important. Content provider companies say that Internet Service Providers resist their requests to move aggressively against websites illegally trafficking in copyrighted material and in shutting down service to illegal downloaders. There is a government-organized working group on Internet governance including both sets of stakeholders but so far no solution has been found.

Sweden

Sweden remains a major contributor to the worldwide problem of Internet piracy. Although the police raid against Pirate Bay (the world's largest Bit Torrent tracker) sent shockwaves through international file-sharing circles, the fact that Pirate Bay was back in operation within a few days casts a shadow over the forceful actions of the Swedish authorities and prospective legal action against the operators is likely to take time. Sweden is also still a host to a large part of the world's "top sites" for piracy and the largest number of DC++ file-sharing hubs and users.

The legislative and enforcement framework in Sweden is generally effective against conventional hard goods piracy but actual enforcement with respect to Internet piracy has been weak. In the last year, however, the Swedish government has repeatedly signaled to police and prosecutors that it wants to step up efforts to curb Internet piracy. The government has also requested that the industry provide legal alternatives to file-sharing, and it has appointed a government commission to look into possibilities to encourage such a development.

In the last year, several cases of illegal distribution of copyrighted material on the Internet have been tried in the Swedish courts. The courts have successfully used existing legislation to sentence defendants for the infringing activities. The Swedish government also is working on strengthening existing laws to make it easier for law enforcement officials to meet evidentiary requirements.

SERVICES BARRIERS

Concerns Related to EU Enlargement

On May 28, 2004, the European Commission notified members of the World Trade Organization of a proposed consolidation of the EU's schedule of specific commitments under the General Agreement on Trade in Services (GATS) pursuant to GATS Article V to reflect both the 1995 accession to the European Union of Austria, Finland, and Sweden, and the 2004 accession of Cyprus, the Czech Republic, Estonia, Hungary, Latvia, Lithuania, Malta, Poland, the Slovak Republic, and Slovenia. As a result of this proposed consolidation, a number of previous GATS commitments by these countries have been modified in a way that may reduce sector-specific or horizontal market access commitments. Although not within the scope of the EU's GATS Article V notification, the EU's consolidation proposal also entails the extension to the new Member States of most-favored nation exemptions reflected in the EU's existing schedule of GATS commitments.

Following GATS rules, which allow a Member to reduce or withdraw commitments provided that they negotiate offsetting compensation to maintain the overall level of market access, the United States closely worked with Brazil, Hong Kong, Japan, Canada and 12 other WTO Members to negotiate a compensation package with the European Union. Negotiations were successfully completed on September 25, 2006. The agreed compensation package contains new and enhanced commitments in several other services sectors, including public utilities, engineering, computer, advertising, and financial services.

Television Broadcast Directive (Television without Frontiers Directive)

The 1989 EU Broadcast Directive (also known as the Television without Frontiers Directive) includes a provision requiring that a majority of television transmission time be reserved for European-origin programs "where practicable and by appropriate means." All EU Member States, including the Member States that acceded to the EU in May 2004 and January 2007, have enacted legislation to implement the Broadcast Directive. It remains important to ensure that the flexibility built into the Directive is preserved and that individual broadcasting markets are allowed to develop according to their specific conditions and needs.

In December, 2005, the European Commission adopted a proposal for revising the Television without Frontiers Directive. The proposal distinguishes between "linear" services (scheduled broadcasting via traditional TV or other means which "pushes" content) and "non-linear" services (such as on-demand films or other news which the viewer "pulls" from a network). TV broadcasting rules would apply to linear services in a modernized, more flexible form, while non-linear services (which are not covered under the 1989 directive) would be subject to a set of basic principles, including the protection of minors and prevention of incitement to racial hatred. The proposal maintains the country of origin principle. The Culture Committee of the European Parliament issued a report on the proposal in August, 2006. The legislation, which requires approval of the European Parliament and Member States, is not expected to be finalized until late 2007 or possibly 2008.

Several EU Member States have specific legislation that hinders the free flow of some programming. A summary of some of the more salient restrictive national practices follows.

France

France continues to apply its more restrictive version of the EU Broadcast Directive which was first introduced into French legislation and approved by the European Commission in 1992. In implementing the Directive, France chose to specify a percentage of European programming (60 percent) and French programming (40 percent) which exceeded the requirements of the Broadcast Directive. Moreover, these quotas apply to both the 24-hour day and prime time slots, and the definition of prime time differs from network to network. The prime time rules are a significant barrier to access of U.S. programs to the French market. In addition, the United States continues to be concerned that radio broadcast quotas which have been in effect since 1996 (40 percent of songs on almost all French private and public radio stations must be Francophone), limit broadcasts of American music.

Italy

Legislation passed in 1998 that made Italy's TV broadcast quota stricter than the EU Broadcast Directive remains in effect. The legislation makes 51 percent European content mandatory during prime time, and excludes talk shows from the programming that may be counted toward fulfilling the quota. A 1998 regulation also requires all multiplex movie theaters of more than 1,300 seats to reserve 15 to 20 percent of their seats, distributed over no fewer than three screens, to showing EU films. In May 2004, Italy enacted controversial media reform through the "Gasparri Law," under which the media/communications market is considered one sector. Under this law, no single operator may receive more than 20 percent of the sector's total revenues. In addition, the law provides for the gradual privatization of RAI, the state-owned radio and television broadcasting conglomerate. The government of Italy is in the process of reconsidering Gasparri Law provisions.

Spain

Spain's theatrical film system has been modified sufficiently in recent years so that it is no longer a major source of trade friction. Government regulations issued in 1997 require exhibitors to show one day of EU-produced film for every three days of non-EU-produced film. Spanish law requires that the quotas issue be reviewed in 2006. The Ministry of Culture is currently preparing a draft Film Law.

Postal Services

United States service and package service providers have in the past expressed concern that postal monopolies in many EU Member States restrict their market access and create unfair conditions of competition with the incumbents.

With the adoption of the Postal Services Directive, the European Union in 1997 took a first step to get national postal monopolies to gradually open up to competition. A second Directive in 2002 succeeded in opening up a number of postal services -- including all outgoing cross-border mail -- but stopped short of liberalizing the market for the delivery of letters weighing less than 50 grams. On October 18, 2006, the European Commission adopted a proposal to open up postal markets to full, unrestricted competition by 2009. The proposal is subject to approval by the Member States and the European Parliament and is expected to go into effect in summer 2007.

Belgium

While the Belgian Post has taken measures in recent years to liberalize, industry competitors continue to express concerns about market access and a postal monopoly operating in Belgium. January 2006 legislation introduced a licensing regime for universal postal services as well as a compensation fund for universal service. The licensing regime would provide revenue to the Belgian Post if liberalization proved unprofitable due to its universal service obligation. Under the current legal framework, express companies appear to be exempt from the licensing regime as well as from the obligation to provide for a compensation fund for universal service on the condition that these services are clearly distinct from the universal postal service by virtue of their value-added characteristics.

Germany

In February 2005, the Federal Regulatory Agency (Bundesnetzagentur) took action against Deutsche Post AG (DPAG), in response to complaints from competitors. Its ruling forbids DPAG from hindering or discriminating against rival small- and medium-sized providers of mail preparation services, especially those collecting and presorting letters and feeding mail items weighing less than 100 grams into DPAG's sorting centers. This ruling follows an October 2004 move by the European Commission to initiate a treaty infringement procedure against Germany for failing to mandate that DPAG offer unbundled access to competitors. Some U.S. companies have indicated they might be interested in providing services such as sorting.

Ireland
Currently, postal services "reserved" to An Post, the national postal agency and Ireland's designated Universal Service Provider, are confined to items of domestic correspondence and incoming cross-border correspondence weighing 50g or less. All mail falling outside this category is open to competition and can be handled by any mail/package company operating in the Irish market. From January 2009, the postal market will be fully open to competition and other operators will be free to handle any mail now reserved to An Post.

Professional Services

In the area of professional services, there are significant variations among EU Member State requirements for foreign lawyers and accountants intending to practice in the European Union. While many of these are not outright barriers, disparities among Member State requirements can complicate access to the European market for U.S. lawyers and accountants.

Legal Services

Austria
U.S. citizens can only provide legal advice on U.S. law and public international law (excluding EU law) on a temporary basis. Only an Austrian or other EU national can join the Bar Association. U.S. nationals cannot represent clients before Austrian courts and authorities, and cannot establish a commercial presence in Austria. However, informal cooperation with Austrian partners is possible.

Czech Republic
The Czech Republic requires that all attorneys be members of the Czech bar. U.S. educated lawyers may register with the Czech Bar and take an equivalency exam, but are limited to practicing home state (U.S.) law and international law. To represent clients in Czech courts, U.S. lawyers must first undergo a three-year legal traineeship and pass the Czech bar exam. U.S. firms are allowed to cooperate with local firms and lend them their name; as a result, firms that operate in the country do so as independent Czech branches. They may have U.S. attorneys that are attached to the staffs as "advisors."

Finland
Foreigners from non-EU countries cannot become members of the Finnish Bar Association and receive the higher law profession title of Asianajaja (Attorney at Law). Persons holding the title of Asianajaja are subject to Asianajaja Law as well as bar regulations. While the title gives added prestige and helps solicit clients, it is not essential to practice domestic or international law or to represent a client in court.

France
Non-EU firms are not permitted to establish branch offices in France under their own names. Also, non-EU lawyers and firms are not permitted to form partnerships with or hire French lawyers.

Germany

U.S. lawyers that have joined the German Bar Association under their home title may practice international law (but not EU law) and the law of their home country. To be admitted to the bar to practice German law, individuals generally have to complete five years of study, then successfully complete the first of two state exams. After successfully completing the first exam they undertake two years of practical training. Individuals then take the second state exam, and upon passing, are admitted to the bar.

Hungary

Foreign non-EU lawyers may provide legal advice on legislation of their own country and international law. Lawyers registered in the EU may be admitted to the bar. Foreign lawyers from non-EU countries may establish a partnership with a Hungarian legal firm and provide legal services under a "cooperation agreement."

Ireland

In general, lawyers with non-Irish qualifications who wish to practice Irish law and appear before Irish courts must either pass transfer examinations or retrain as lawyers under the direction of the Law Society of Ireland. Only lawyers who have either been admitted to the Bar of England, Wales, or Northern Ireland, practiced as an attorney in New York, California, Pennsylvania (with five years experience required in Pennsylvania), or New Zealand, or have been admitted as lawyers in either an EU or EFTA Member State are entitled to take the transfer examination.

Italy

In 2001, Italy passed a law implementing EU Directive 98/5 on EU lawyers' freedom to establish themselves EU-wide and enabling Italian lawyers to practice jointly, including with EU lawyers, through a limited liability partnership or through the Italian branch of a partnership formed in another EU Member State, as long as the limited liability partnership is composed exclusively of Italian and EU lawyers. The status of non-EU lawyers is not explicitly addressed by the law. This omission leaves the status of international law firms with offices in Italy uncertain, insofar as they have Italian and non-EU lawyers as partners. Despite this ambiguity, several major U.S. law firms have a presence in Italy.

Lithuania

Only EU citizens may join the Lithuanian bar and establish law firms that provide the full range of legal services. Lithuanian law permits U.S. attorneys to establish law offices that provide paralegal services. These firms differ from traditional law firms, however, in that they cannot compel Lithuanian institutions to provide information, nor can they protect legally the lawyer-client privilege.

U.S. firms can, however, easily partner with a local law firm to provide a full range of legal services.

Slovakia

In August 2006, the Slovak Antimonopoly Office overturned Act No. 586/2003 (the Advocacy Act) which was designed to force non-EU-based law firms to change their legal status from a branch partnership to a limited liability company (LLC). Under the Advocacy

Act, an LLC had to be owned by an EU advocate registered in Slovakia or a Slovak national, and non-EU law firms could not market themselves under their internationally recognized corporate identities, incurring extra costs to comply with the special rules. The ruling also overturned the Slovak Bar's internal rules that restrict a firm's name to that of living partners. The Slovak Antimonopoly Office found that the rules contravened Article 81 of the Founding Treaty of the European Community, as well as Slovakia's own Act on the Protection of Economic Competition.

The Slovak law still requires non-EU-based lawyers and law firms to register with the Slovak Bar Association to practice law in Slovakia. In 2006, no U.S. attorneys have been able to register. The United States is concerned that the Slovak Bar consistently has tried to limit foreign lawyers' ability to practice law in Slovakia; this provision of the Advocacy Act appears to facilitate its ability to deny foreign lawyers registration.

Accounting and Auditing Services

France
There is a nationality requirement for the establishment of a practice, which can be waived at the discretion of the French authorities. An applicant for such a permit, however, must have lived in France for at least five years.

Greece
U.S. access to the Greek accounting market remains limited. A 1997 Presidential decree established a method for fixing minimum fees for audits and established restrictions on the use of different types of personnel in audits. It also prohibited auditing firms from doing multiple tasks for a client, thus raising the cost of audit work. The Greek government has defended these regulations as necessary to ensure the quality and objectivity of audits.

Hungary
Only Hungarian-certified accountants may conduct audits, but this individual may work for a foreign-owned firm.

Architectural Services

The U.S. National Council for Architectural Registration Boards and the EU Architect's Council of Europe signed a joint recommendation for a Mutual Recognition Agreement for Architects in November 2005. The U.S. Government and the European Commission will collaborate with relevant regulators and professional associations to consider options for the promotion of progress towards such an agreement in accordance with each side's legal systems.

Austria
Only citizens from EU and EEA Member States are eligible to obtain a license to provide independent architectural services in Austria. This restriction does not appear to be reflected in the European Communities' Schedule of Specific Commitments under the GATS.

Financial Services

Poland
Citibank and other service providers have requested that the Polish government treat independent legal persons as a single taxable person as allowed by the EU VAT Directive. VAT grouping is already employed by the UK, the Netherlands, Ireland, Germany, Austria, Denmark, Finland and Sweden. VAT grouping would allow financial service providers to recover VAT charges they incur upon making intra-company payments for supplies, including labor costs.

Telecommunications Market Access

Both the WTO commitments covering telecommunications services and the EU's Common Regulatory Framework for Electronic Communications Networks and Services (Framework Directive), have encouraged liberalization and competition in the European telecommunications sector. As part of the WTO Agreement, for example, all EU Member States made commitments to provide market access and national treatment for voice telephony and data services. The Framework Directive imposes additional liberalization and harmonization requirements, and the Commission has taken action against Member States that have not implemented the Framework Directive. However, implementation of these requirements has been uneven across Member States and in many markets significant problems remain, including with the provisioning and pricing of unbundled local loops, line sharing, co-location, and the provisioning of leased lines. Partial government ownership of some Member States' incumbent telecommunications operators also has the potential to raise problems for new entrants.

In 2002, the EU issued a new regulatory framework for electronic communications that includes the EU Framework Directive and four specific Directives on: (1) licensing; (2) access and interconnection; (3) universal service and user rights; and (4) data protection.

This new regulatory framework requires Member States to update and adapt legislation to account for converging technologies and for future technological and market developments. It applies to all forms of electronic communications networks and associated services, not just traditional fixed telephony networks. The long-term goal is to phase out sector-specific, *ex-ante* regulation (for all but public interest reasons) in favor of reliance on general competition rules.

Beginning in December 2005, the European Commission began a process of reviewing the directives under the regulatory framework for electronic communications, and the European Commission is expected to make proposals for revising the directives in mid-2007.

Member State Practices
Enforcement of existing legislation by the National Regulating Authorities (NRAs) has been hampered by unnecessarily lengthy and cumbersome procedures in France, Italy, Austria, and Portugal, among others. The European Commission has also found that incumbents in Germany, Greece, Spain, Italy, Ireland, Austria, Finland, and Sweden have slowed the arrival of competition by systematically appealing their national regulators' decisions.

Austria

In general, Austria has moved toward a more open and competitive telecommunications market and has implemented the relevant directives. There are several outstanding concerns related to: (1) the unbundling of the "last mile," (2) deficient procedures for the wholesale broadband access market (including bitstream access), (3) problems with the wholesale line rental, (4) interconnection fees and (5) the market for public telecommunications transit services. Generally, Austria's NRA – the TKC – provides timely initial decisions, but follow-up on those decisions, including the appeals process for such decisions, remains uncertain and slow.

Finland

Finland has one of the most mature mobile markets in Europe, with overall penetration rates in 2006 above the EU average. Fierce competition and a tough regulatory environment have created a difficult market for mobile operators. Finland has the third lowest mobile call charges of all Member States, behind only Denmark and Luxemburg. The merger of Telia and Sonera in 2002 reduced the number of competitors, since Telia in consequence relinquished its Finnish mobile business, and in late 2005 Tele2 also withdrew.

Finnish mobile phone operators have slowed the arrival of competition by systematically appealing the Finnish NRA – Finnish Communications Regulatory Authority FICORA's SMP (significant market power) decisions. The appeal processes have played an important role in the effectiveness of regulation in Finland, and appeals can take several years. Recent cases from Finland, where appeals have taken as long as three to five years, underscore the fact that the current system creates a high degree of regulatory uncertainty.

France

French cell phone usage is finally catching up to the European average, topping 80 percent penetration in 2006.

France implemented the EU Framework Directive in 2004, and the NRA (ARCEP) has made some progress in subsequently conducting the required market analyses of telecommunications sectors.

France Telecom (FT) was fined 80 million euros in July 2006 by a French Court of Appeals, which had found the company abused its position as France's dominant telecommunications operator by blocking access for rival ADSL Internet operators to its network between 1999 and 2002. The appeals court upheld an earlier decision by the French Competition Council, which has been playing an increasingly important role in the telecommunications sector as France Telecom struggles to maintain its dominant position. FT's domination is no longer a given as innovative technologies are deployed to offer "triple play" (long distance, Internet, and television) and even "four play" (triple play plus mobile telephone) packages at cut rate prices.

Germany

Germany has made slow progress in introducing competition to some sectors of its telecommunications market. The revised Telecommunications Act entered into force in June 2004 and most competitors to DT believe that it should facilitate enhanced competition. New entrants report they continue to face difficulties competing with the partially state-owned incumbent Deutsche Telekom AG (DT), which retains a near-monopoly in a number of key services, including local loop and broadband connections. On the positive side, greater competition for local and long-distance calling has helped competitors gain more than 20 percent of the local calling market since 2003. Currently, the National Regulatory Agency is studying how it should regulate 18 individual market segments, as required by the Framework Directive. After more than a year, it has completed twelve market studies.

In 2006, the German government amended the Telecommunications Act to boost customer protection rules, including more transparent pricing and billing, and introduce liability limitations for service providers. Section 9a of the amended Act, which took effect in February 2007, may grant "regulatory holidays" for services in new markets. DT has lobbied hard for such an exemption; competitors complain that Section 9a will shield DT from regulation as it installs a lucrative fiber optic network in order to provide triple play services. Since DT lacks a significant competitor capable of making a similar offering, this provision risks creating a *de facto* monopoly for services which do not meet the criteria of a "new market." The U.S. Government has raised serious concerns and engaged the German government repeatedly on this issue. The European Commissioner for Information Society initiated infringement proceedings immediately after Section 9a entered into force.

Companies have complained that DT and other mobile providers charge excessive termination rates when fixed-line users call mobile phones. After a June 2004 voluntary agreement by mobile operators failed to reduce termination charges and under continued EU pressure, the Federal Network Agency directed mobile providers in August 2006 to lower termination charges to a cost-based level. In addition, in October 2005, in response to complaints by competitors, the National Regulatory Agency launched a probe into whether DT is violating its dominant market position with the offer of a new low-cost ISDN Internet connection subscription fee. In September 2006, it issued a ruling requiring DT to grant competitors, upon request, IP bitstream access to residential customers, such as unbundled broadband access based on the Internet protocol.

Hungary

The Hungarian telecommunications market is almost fully liberalized. However, legal obstacles, as well as a lack of investors, have hindered competition. In May 2005, following the general policy of majority owner Deutsche Telekom (DT), the Hungarian "T-Brands" (Axelero, the Internet service provider; the business solutions branch; and the cable provider branch) merged with Matáv, the former monopolist and today's market-leading telephony provider, under the name of Magyar Telekom Rt. In October 2005, Magyar Telekom Rt. merged with T-Mobile Hungary, the leading mobile phone operator, which is also partially owned by DT. This involved changes in management and strengthened Magyar Telekom's leading position in the voice and communications market. UPC and TELE2, as new-fixed line providers, launched their services offering lower tariffs than Matav. In addition, UPC has focused on bundling television, broadband Internet and telephony services to gain larger market share in an ever-shrinking fixed-line telephony environment. The number of fixed line subscriptions decreased to 33.8 percent by the end of the second quarter of 2006, while mobile phone penetration continues to increase, reaching nearly 94 percent at the end of the same quarter.

Ireland

The government privatized the state monopoly, Telecom Eireann, in 1999, and the new company, Eircom, retains a 74 percent share of the fixed lines in Ireland and dominates leased-line services and national interconnection, entailing high prices for local services. Competition in the Irish communications market intensified in 2006, with an ever-growing number of authorised operators. There were also several high-profile mergers and acquisitions, notably the purchase of a majority stake in Eircom by Australia-based Babcock and Brown in June 2006. There are four mobile operators active in the Irish market. As of June 2006, the mobile penetration rate in Ireland was 103 percent, with 4.37 million mobile subscribers.

Broadband use has grown with an increase in the number of licensed operators. Broadband penetration was estimated at 8.8 percent in June 2006, up from 5 percent in 2005. Ireland has adopted EU local loop unbundling (LLU) legislation, and the government has initiated legal action to compel Eircom to complete LLU in order to promote competition and innovation in the DSL market.

Luxembourg

In 2005, Luxembourg began revising administrative procedures to implement the EU Framework Directive to liberalize Member States' telecommunications markets and allow for fairer competition. Despite these efforts, the state-owned P and T company continues to dominate the nation's telecommunications market. In addition, despite a 1998 court ruling opening Luxembourg's small mobile phone market to competition, the wireless communications market remains dominated by only three companies, one of which is half-owned by the state company.

Poland

Telecommunications and Internet investments remain strong in Poland. New competitors (Netia, Orange, Germanos) have entered the cellular market, and well-known Internet presences, such as Google, are locating in Warsaw. Still, the ability of new entrants to compete may have been hindered by the failure of Poland's Electronic Communications Office – UKE – to implement the EU Framework Directive in a timely manner. The UKE continues to battle Polish telecommunications operator TPSA over its monopolistic business practices.

Spain

Access to leased lines in Spain remains problematic because rates do not appear to be based on actual cost. Despite actions by CMT, Spain's NRA, wholesale prices are still above the European average and approximately 100 percent above U.S. prices. This has allowed the incumbent operator Telefónica to offer services to customers at substantially lower rates than competitive carriers.

U.S. companies have complained that Spanish mobile operators are charging excessively high mobile termination rates and that they are squeezed out of the fixed-to-mobile communications market because mobile operators offer their subscribers mobile-to-mobile and fixed-to-mobile calls at below wholesale rates. Spanish anti-trust authorities are considering penalizing these mobile operators.

Evolution of the broadband market has been slow and problematic, and many operators have ceased offering these services. However, Telefónica's market share is being challenged by two operators: Ya.com and Wanadoo. Both of these companies have established partnerships with Spanish fixed and mobile line carriers.

INVESTMENT BARRIERS

Overview

The European Commission's mandate on investment issues is evolving. EU Member States negotiate their own bilateral investment protection and taxation treaties and generally retain responsibility for their investment regimes. In many areas, individual Member State policies and practices have a more significant impact on U.S. firms than do EU-level policies and practices.

Under the 1993 Maastricht Treaty, free movement of capital became an EU responsibility and capital controls both among EU Member States and between EU members and third countries were lifted. A few Member States' barriers remain in place, although in particular cases, EU law may supersede these. Right of establishment issues, particularly regarding third countries, are a shared competence between the EU and the Member States. The division of this shared competence varies from sector to sector based on whether the EU has issued regulations in a particular sector. Direct branches of non-EU financial service institutions remain subject to individual Member State authorization and regulation.

The EU requires national treatment for foreign investors in most sectors. EU law, with a few exceptions, requires that any company established under the laws of one Member State must, as a Community undertaking, receive national treatment in all Member States, regardless of its ultimate ownership. However, some restrictions on U.S. investment do exist under EU law and others have been proposed, as discussed below.

Ownership Restrictions and Reciprocity Provisions

EU Treaty Articles 43 (establishment) and 56/57 (capital movements) have helped the EU to achieve one of the most hospitable climates for U.S. investment in the world, but some restrictions on foreign direct investment remain in place. Under EU law, the right to provide aviation transport services within the EU is reserved to firms majority-owned and controlled by EU nationals. The right to provide maritime transport services within certain EU Member States is also restricted. EU banking, insurance and investment services directives currently include "reciprocal" national treatment clauses under which a financial services firm from a third country may be denied the right to establish a new business in the EU if the EU determines that the investor's home country denies national treatment to EU service providers. The right of U.S. firms to national treatment in this area was reinforced by the EU's GATS commitments.

After years of discussion, the Council of Ministers finally agreed in March 2004 on a directive on takeover bids ("Takeover Directive"). The original proposal would have banned any national legislation allowing companies to prevent hostile takeovers through the use of defensive measures (e.g., "poison pills" or multiple voting rights). The final directive makes it optional for Member States and companies to maintain a regime that rules out these defensive measures or to opt out of such rules. The European Parliament debated whether to limit the benefits of the new directive to companies that apply the same provisions, (*e.g.*, limiting the right of a board to take defensive measures or to mitigate the role of restrictions on share transfers or voting in a takeover bid). Article 12.3 of the final text is ambiguous as to whether the limitation would apply to non-EU firms, although the preamble of the legislation states that the application of the optional measures is without prejudice to international agreements to which the EC is a party.

The Directive was due to be implemented by the Member States by May 20, 2006. However, only Denmark, France, Hungary, Luxembourg, and the UK met this deadline. Ireland and Germany implemented the Directive after the deadline, and other countries have introduced draft legislation.

Under the 1994 hydrocarbons directive (Directive 94/22/EC), an investor may be denied a license to explore for and exploit hydrocarbon resources if the investor's home country does not permit EU investors to engage in those activities under circumstances "comparable" to those in the EU. These reciprocity provisions thus far have not affected any U.S.-owned firms.

Member State Practices

Austria

While European Economic Area (EEA) Member States' banks may operate branches on the basis of their home country licenses, banks from outside the EEA must obtain Austrian licenses to operate in Austria. However, if a non-EEA bank has already obtained a license in another EEA country for the operation of a subsidiary, it does not need a license to establish branch offices in Austria.

Bulgaria

Local companies in which foreign partners have controlling interests must obtain licenses to engage in certain activities, including: production and export of arms/ammunition; banking and insurance; exploration, development, and exploitation of natural resources; and acquisition of property in certain geographic areas. On February 23, 2007, the United States and Bulgaria signed the Treaty on Avoidance of Double Taxation (DTT). The U.S. business community in Bulgaria believes that the DTT will facilitate bilateral investment and trade. The insolvency rules in Bulgaria's Commercial Code and its Law on Public Offering of Securities (2005) have greatly improved the legislative protection for minority shareholders, but enforcement of the law's provisions is inadequate and corporate governance remains weak.

Cyprus

Property Acquisition: Cypriot law imposes significant restrictions on the foreign ownership of real property. Persons not ordinarily resident in Cyprus (whether of EU or non-EU origin) may purchase only a single piece of real estate (not to exceed three donum or roughly one acre) for private use (normally a holiday home). Exceptions can be made for projects requiring larger plots of land (i.e., beyond that necessary for a private residence) but they are difficult to obtain and are rarely granted. The restriction on property acquisition for EU citizens not normally resident in Cyprus will expire in May 2009. (Cyprus received a temporary derogation from the EU *acquis communautaire* on this issue, lasting for five years after accession). The restrictions will continue to apply, however, to non-EU residents, including U.S. nationals.

Tertiary education investment restrictions: Cypriot legislation on foreign investment in tertiary education distinguishes between colleges and universities. Investment in universities, defined as institutions with no fewer than 1,000 students enrolled in a sufficiently diverse range of classes and curricula, is encouraged. Foreign (including non-EU) investors can set up or acquire a university in Cyprus by simply registering a company on the island and following a set of non-discriminatory criteria. By contrast, non-EU investment in colleges is discouraged. Non-EU investors can set up or acquire a local college by registering a company in Cyprus or elsewhere in the EU provided that the company has EU-origin shareholders and directors. As a consequence, non-EU investors are not allowed to participate whether as directors or shareholders in the administration of local colleges.

Investment Restriction in Media Companies: Cyprus also restricts non-EU ownership of local mass media companies to 5 percent or less for individual investors and 25 percent or less for all foreign investors in each individual media company.

Construction: Under the Registration and Control of Contractors Laws of 2001 and 2004, the right to register as a construction contractor in Cyprus is reserved for citizens of EU Member States. Non-EU entities are not allowed to own a majority stake in a local construction company. Non-EU physical persons or legal entities may bid on specific construction projects, but only after obtaining a special license by the Council of Ministers.

Professional Recognition of Real Estate Agents and Other Groups: The current law licensing real estate agents to practice in Cyprus, last amended in 2003, acts as a protectionist measure, creating significant barriers to entry into the profession. Cypriot law recognizes only licensed individuals (not companies) to act as authorized real estate entities and licenses are only granted to individuals who have served as apprentices to licensed individuals for up to eight years. Existing real estate agents have also tried to use the law to restrict the ability of foreign real estate networks to advertise in their own names, although this interpretation of the law is under debate. There are also similar concerns about the transparency of the legislation concerning state recognition and accreditation of several other professions, including medical doctors and civil aviation pilots.

France

There are generally few screening or prior approval requirements for non-EU foreign investment in France. As part of a November 2004 law that streamlined the French Monetary and Financial Code, however, the State Council was directed to define a number of sensitive sectors in which prior approval would be required before acquisition of an equity stake.

A December 2005 government decree lists 11 business sectors in which the French Ministry of Economy, Finance and Industry has the right to monitor and restrict foreign ownership through a system of "prior authorization." These sectors include: businesses involved in the gambling industry, regulated businesses providing private security services, businesses involved in the research and development or manufacture of means of fighting the illegal use of pathogens or toxic substances by terrorists and preventing the adverse health-related consequences of such use, businesses dealing with wiretapping and mail interception equipment, businesses licensed to audit and certify services relating to the security of information technology systems and products, businesses providing goods and services relating to the security of the information systems of public or private-sector companies managing critical infrastructures, and businesses relating to certain dual-use items and technology.

The GOF is working on a draft bill on the protection from foreign takeover bids of 20 French companies defined as "sensitive." In addition, the government implemented the EU anti-takeover directive on March 31, 2006. Implementing legislation allows companies to resort to a U.S. style "poison pill" takeover defense, including granting existing shareholders and employees the right to increase their leverage by buying more shares through stock purchase warrants at a discount in case of an unwanted takeover. The government also asked the state-owned financial institution Caisse de Depots et Consignations (CDC), France's largest institutional investor, to work as a domestic buffer against foreign takeovers by increasing its stakes in French companies. In the name of "economic patriotism," the French government has thus demonstrated an inclination to intervene in potential transnational mergers or to otherwise signal its interest in defending French commercial "champions" from foreign takeover attempts.

Germany

Germany's 2002 takeover law was marginally changed by the implementation of the EU takeover directive. Germany made use of its "opt-out" right and retained measures that allow firms to ward off hostile takeover bids, first at the shareholder level, where management may be given authority at annual shareholder meetings to take necessary measures to guard against unwanted takeover interest; and, second, at the management level, where the managing board may take protective measures upon approval by the supervisory board, bypassing the need for shareholder approval altogether. The EU directive offers companies the choice either to abide by the German law or to "opt-in" to the EU regulation. Companies using the "opt-in" may limit their waiver of Germany's protective measures to companies that also have no measures in place to fend-off hostile takeover bids.

Germany passed legislation in July 2004 requiring notification by foreign entities of investments expected to exceed 25 percent of the equity of German firms engaged in the production of armaments and cryptology technology used for classified government communications. Following an inter-ministerial review, the government may veto such sales within one month of receipt of a notification. The German government expanded the scope of the law in 2005 to include tank and tracked vehicle engines to block a U.S. financial investor from buying a tank engine manufacturer.

Greece

Greek authorities consider local content and export performance when evaluating applications for tax and investment incentives. Such criteria do not appear to be prerequisites for approving investments, however.

Greece has opened its telecommunications market and is in the process of gradually liberalizing its energy sector. At present, however, Greece's inhospitable regulatory framework has hampered efforts by U.S. firms to develop energy production facilities.

U.S. and other non-EU investors receive less advantageous treatment in Greece than domestic or other EU competitors in the banking, mining, maritime, air transport and broadcast industries (which were opened to EU citizens under EU single market rules). For reasons of national security, non-EU investors are restricted in their ability to purchase land in border regions and on certain islands.

Italy

The EU Takeover Directive has not yet been incorporated into Italian law. Current Italian law, which continues to apply pending the enactment in Italy of the EU Directive, requires the target of a takeover or merger bid to obtain authorization from shareholders before undertaking defensive measures to fend off a hostile bid and provides for a break-through rule on the most common pre-bid defensive tactics (i.e., shareholder voting agreements).

With few exceptions, Italy provides national treatment to foreign investors established in Italy or in another EU member state, as required by Article 43 of the EU Treaty. Under current regulations, U.S. and other non-Italian banks must obtain Bank of Italy approval to operate in Italy. Foreign banks face the same capital requirements as banks chartered in Italy. U.S. and other investment firms from non-EU countries may operate with authorization from Italy's securities market regulator, CONSOB. CONSOB may deny authorization to investment firms from countries that discriminate against Italian firms.

Malta

Maltese law requires that anyone buying residential or commercial real estate must obtain a permit from the Minister of Finance. EU citizens and returning Maltese migrants who have lived in Malta for more than five years receive a waiver from these permits. Non-EU citizens are not entitled to this waiver. Despite the restriction, permission to purchase land for commercial or residential purposes is normally granted. No U.S. businesses appear to have been discouraged from investing in Malta because of these restrictions. The restrictions have, however, delayed certain business investment projects involving American businesses.

Romania

A law on securities that was passed in 2004 entitles majority shareholders owning 95 percent of the total stock in a firm to buy residual shares. This law is considered to be a compromise, and provides very limited minority shareholder protection. Some minority shareholders have complained that Romanian authorities do not adequately protect their rights. A continued impediment to foreign investment is Romania's inconsistent legal and regulatory system. Tax laws change frequently and are unevenly enforced. Tort cases often require lengthy, expensive procedures, and judges' rulings are often not enforced.

ELECTRONIC COMMERCE

U.S. businesses and the U.S. Government continue to monitor potential problems related to data privacy regulation and legal liabilities for companies doing business over the Internet in the EU.

Data Privacy

The EU Data Protection Directive (1995/46) allows the transmission of EU data to third countries only if those countries are deemed by the European Commission to provide an adequate level of protection by reason of its domestic law or of the international commitments it has entered into (Article 25(6)). U.S. companies can only receive or transfer employee and customer information from the EU by using one of the exceptions to the Directive's adequacy requirements or by demonstrating they can provide adequate protection for the transferred data. These requirements can be burdensome for many U.S. industries that rely on data exchange across the Atlantic.

Currently, the Commission has recognized Switzerland, Canada, Argentina, Guernsey, Isle of Man, the U.S. Department of Commerce's Safe Harbor Privacy Principles, and the transfer of Air Passenger Name Record to the U.S. Bureau of Customs and Border Protection as providing adequate protection. The U.S. Safe Harbor framework provides U.S. companies with a simple, streamlined means of complying with the adequacy requirement. The agreement allows U.S. companies that commit to a series of data protection principles (based on the Directive) and that publicly state their commitment by "self-certifying" on a dedicated website (www.export.gov/safeharbor), to continue to receive and transfer personal data from the EU. Signing up to the Safe Harbor is voluntary, but the rules are binding on signatories. A failure to fulfill the commitments of the Safe Harbor framework is actionable either as an unfair and deceptive practice under Section 5 of the FTC Act or, for air carriers and ticket agents, under a concurrent Department of Transportation statute.

The U.S. Government actively supports the Safe Harbor framework and encourages the European Commission and Member States to continue to use the flexibility offered by the Data Protection Directive to avoid unnecessary interruptions in data flows to the United States. Furthermore, the U.S. Government expects the European Commission and EU Member States to fulfill their commitment to inform the U.S. Government if they become aware of any actions that may interrupt data flows to the United States.

Brussels Regulation

On December 22, 2000, the EU adopted the so-called Brussels Regulation which allows consumers to sue companies in the court of their country of residence, "when the website is directed to [his/her] Member State or to several countries, including that Member State." Industry has complained that the practical effect of this regulation is that companies doing business on the Internet in the EU risk being sued in every EU Member State, as opposed to being subject to the jurisprudence of their country of origin.

OTHER BARRIERS

Healthcare

Ireland

U.S. healthcare firms have faced difficulties entering Ireland's hybrid public-private health system. To generate sufficient revenues to justify investments in Irish hospitals and equipment, U.S. firms usually seek to treat both private and public patients. The treatment of public patients, however, requires a Service Level Agreement from the Health Service Executive (HSE), the administrative agency that oversees Ireland's hospital system. U.S. firms report difficulties in securing such an agreement from the HSE, despite longstanding problems with the provision of public health services in Ireland.

In the health insurance market, Ireland has espoused "risk equalization," whereby private insurers are required by law to compensate the Voluntary Health Insurance (VHI) Board, a quasi-governmental body, for the additional risk that it accepts in offering community (or equal) rating for policy-holders of different ages and medical profiles. Compensation is to be paid once a certain threshold based on the number of insured is reached, but the Irish government has not clarified the formula for determining the threshold. This ambiguity has been a factor in discouraging U.S. insurance firms from entering the Irish market.

In: Trade Barriers in Europe
Editor: Paula R. Lignelli, pp. 59-68

ISBN: 978-1-60021-956-6
© 2007 Nova Science Publishers, Inc.

Chapter 2

KENYA

TRADE SUMMARY

The U.S. goods trade surplus with Kenya was $172 million in 2006, a decrease of $112 million from $284 million in 2005. U.S. goods exports in 2006 were $526 million, down 16.8 percent from the previous year. Corresponding U.S. imports from Kenya were $354 million, up 1.6 percent. Kenya is currently the 82nd largest export market for U.S. goods.

The stock of U.S. foreign direct investment in Kenya in 2005 was $89 million (latest data available), up from $86 million.

IMPORT POLICIES

Tariffs

Kenya is a Member of the World Trade Organization (WTO), the Free Trade Area of the Common Market for Eastern and Southern Africa (COMESA), and the East African Community (EAC). High import duties and Kenya's value-added tax (VAT) pose trade barriers, especially in the agricultural sector. Kenya's import regulations on agricultural products are sometimes altered to reflect fluctuations in domestic supply and demand as well as political factors. The government continues to carefully control imports of seed corn by subjecting hybrid varieties to a certification process that effectively restricts trade.

With the establishment on January 1, 2005 of the EAC Customs Union (between Kenya, Uganda, and Tanzania), the government established three tariff bands: zero duty for raw materials and inputs; 10 percent for processed or manufactured inputs; and 25 percent for finished products. According to the WTO, the move from national tariffs to a common external tariff under the EAC reduced average tariff protection in Kenya. A selected list of sensitive items, comprising 58 tariff lines, was assigned rates above 25 percent, including milk and milk products, corn, rice, wheat and wheat flour. (Wheat flour is imported duty-free from member states of COMESA and the EAC.) Tree nuts, including almonds, are not classified under the sensitive products list but experienced an increase in duty. The tariff on unshelled almonds increased from zero percent to 10 percent, and shelled almonds and other nuts increased from 15 percent to 25 percent. The duty on used clothing, a major U.S. export to the EAC region, was increased to 45 percent or $0.30 per kilogram, whichever is higher. While the U.S. Government welcomed the simplification of the tariff system that came about as a result of the EAC Customs Union, it has raised concerns with Kenya and other EAC members about exceptional tariff increases on used clothing, as well as higher tariffs on almonds and some other U.S. exports to the region.

In 2004, the government introduced an export tax on hides, skins, and scrap metal to encourage local processing rather than the export of these items. Refrigerated trucks and hotel equipment received duty exemptions.

In June 2006 the government eliminated import duties on solar equipment and accessories, bicycle kits, kaolin and kaolinic clays, coke fuel, filter paper, wire of stainless steel and nickel bars, and circular interwoven discs and netting glass fiber. Additionally, import duties were reduced from 25 percent to 10 percent for unassembled kits for motorcycles and unprinted aluminum foil, while duties were increased from 10 percent to 25 percent for floor coverings and mats and from 35 percent to 50 percent on matches.

The government sometimes appears to use the VAT to support policy priorities, both to protect "strategic" sectors such as transportation and agriculture and to address short-term needs. For example, in June 2006, Kenya eliminated the VAT on pharmaceuticals; wheat flour; computer equipment, parts and accessories; liquid petroleum and coal; sanitary pads, baby diapers, napkins, and feeding bottles; supply and treatment of natural water; tractor tires, agricultural tractors, and semi-trailers; and transportation of unprocessed agricultural produce and raw materials such as cut flowers, unroasted coffee, green tea, raw sugar cane, cereals, un-ginned cotton, raw or smoked tobacco and raw pyrethrum.

Non-Tariff Measures

Kenya has removed most non-tariff measures. Those import controls still in existence are based on health, environmental, and security concerns. All Kenyan imports are required to have the following documents: import declaration forms (IDF), a clean report of findings from the Pre-shipment Verification of Conformity agent for regulated products (see Standards section), and valid *pro forma* invoices from the exporting firm.

Kenyan law limits the importation of refined petroleum products by stipulating that any consignment of oil that a company imports for the domestic market be 70 percent crude, thus requiring that it be refined by the Kenya Petroleum Refineries. A senior private sector manager estimates the cost of petroleum products refined in Kenya is about $0.14/gallon higher than imported products, costing Kenyan consumers almost $70 million per year. Oil imports en route to other countries are not affected by this requirement.

Customs Procedures

Kenya is a party to the WTO Customs Valuation Agreement and uses the transaction value for valuation of goods imported from other WTO signatories. Concerns have been raised, however, that this system is not applied consistently. Kenya's customs procedures are detailed and rigidly implemented, often leading to delays in clearance of both imports and exports. In September 2005, the Kenya Revenue Authority (KRA) introduced a new electronic clearing system at the Port of Mombasa, Kenya's major port of entry for imports. Initially, poor implementation, capacity constraints, and information sharing problems created significant delays for some importers. The two private sector firms that administer Kenya's Pre-shipment Verification of Conformity regime (Intertek Testing International and Societe Generale de Surveillance) have been charged with ensuring that up-to-date customs valuation and risk assessment methods are applied.

STANDARDS, TESTING, LABELING AND CERTIFICATION

On September 29, 2005, the government introduced a new Pre-shipment Verification of Conformity (PVC) program. Under the new system, all goods entering the country require a Certificate of Conformity from the country of origin, demonstrating conformity to Kenyan standards. For consignments shipped without inspections, importers may apply for a destination inspection subject to acceptance by the Kenya Bureau of Standards' (KEBS). KEBS is a regulatory body under the Ministry of Trade and Industry. For destination inspection, Kenya requires the importer to pay a 15 percent penalty charge and post a 15 percent bond on the CIF (cost, insurance, freight) value in addition to paying the costs of the test.

Commercial and research applications of agricultural biotechnology in Kenya are currently regulated through guidelines that are neither formal regulations nor enacted law. The guidelines, initially published in 1998 and reviewed yearly, describe a committee-based approach for review and approval of agricultural biotechnology imports, including specific review of end uses (e.g., planting seeds for trials). Substantial quantities of agricultural biotechnology products have been imported into Kenya for food aid purposes since the establishment of the National Biosafety Committee, and significant volumes of food products derived from agricultural biotechnology crops are available commercially. Kenya also imports maize from South Africa, where biotechnology varieties are commercially available.

On September 28, 2006, the Cabinet approved a "National Biotechnology Development Policy 2006" document, which signaled the government's positive attitude toward the use of biotechnology. A draft Biosafety Bill has also been presented to the Cabinet and signed by the Minister of Science and Technology. Although there is momentum in favor of the bill, its actual enactment remains uncertain. As of mid-March 2007, it had yet to be brought before Parliament for debate. Kenya is a party to the Cartagena Protocol on Biosafety.

The Kenya Plant Health Inspectorate Service (KEPHIS), a regulatory agency for quality control, subjects certain imported agricultural goods to further inspection. The Inspectorate also regulates the import and export of plant materials and trade in biotechnology items that require special handling to ensure they are not accidentally released into the environment. KEPHIS evaluates commercial hybrid grain seeds for a period of three years before the seeds can be released to market. According to industry representatives, the certification process can be tedious and restrictive, and the three-year period needed for the government to approve or reject a variety is burdensome. The Ministry of Agriculture restricts cereal seed imports by setting quantitative ceilings. However, once a variety is certified, the quantitative restrictions are lifted.

Any plant consignment arriving in Kenya should have a copy of the plant import permit provided by KEPHIS and an additional health certificate (a phytosanitary certificate), international model, or its equivalent. U.S.-origin genetically modified products must indicate genetic modification status as an additional declaration, with the details stated on the phytosanitary certificate, or they must have a certificate of analysis from a credible laboratory.

GOVERNMENT PROCUREMENT

Kenya is not a signatory to the WTO Agreement on Government Procurement. However, in 2005, Kenya enacted the Public Procurement and Disposal Act, which provides for a Public Procurement Oversight Authority. The Authority entered into force on January 1, 2006, but certain elements of its implementation remain uncertain. Its nine-member Oversight Advisory Board is appointed by the Minister of Finance.

The Public Procurement and Disposal Act is designed to make procurement more transparent and accountable, requiring procurement agencies to carry out an annual update of pre-qualified firms, especially when dealing with restricted tenders, such as security-related tenders. The act establishes penalties for violations of the law, with penalties for individuals up to Ksh4 million (approximately $53,000) in fines, or imprisonment for three years, or both; and for corporations, fines of up to Ksh10 million (approximately $133,300). The Act gives exclusive preferences to Kenyan citizens where the funding is 100 percent from the government of Kenya or a Kenyan body and the amounts are below a yet-to-be determined threshold. The law allows for restricted tendering under certain conditions, such as when the complex or specialized nature of the goods or services limits the competition to pre-qualified contractors. Restrictions can also be imposed if the time and costs required to examine and evaluate a large number of tenders would be disproportionate to the value of the tender. It is uncertain whether the new law will enhance the transparency of national security-related procurements, which have been the subject of a number of high-profile corruption cases in recent years.

The government has taken steps to increase transparency in its public procurement process by removing from its tender documentation a clause that read: "The government reserves the right to accept or reject any bid and is not obliged to give any reasons for its decisions." The Central Tender Board now publishes its decisions and, if a bidder asks, provides the reasons for rejecting certain bids.

In May 2006, the Supplies Management and Practitioners Bill of 2006 was tabled in Parliament for debate. The bill, yet to be passed, aims to complement the Public Procurement and Disposal Act of 2005 by specifying that only a procurement professional may be entrusted with the responsibility of procurement in any public entity.

The World Bank, International Monetary Fund, European Union, and other donors have conditioned some of their official assistance programs, including direct budget support, on reform of public procurement. The donor community hopes the revised public procurement laws will improve Kenya's public procurement system, which has been frequently marred by flawed contracts, awards to noncompetitive firms, and awards to firms in which government officials have a significant interest. Kenya's conflict-ofinterest regulations are often compromised and rarely enforced.

EXPORT SUBSIDIES

Kenya maintains a Manufacturing Under Bond (MUB) program that is designed to encourage manufacturing for export. MUB goods are expected to be exported. If not, they are subject to a surcharge of 2.5 percent and are subject to all other duties. The program is open to both local and foreign investors. Enterprises operating under the program are exempted from duty and VAT on imported raw materials and other imported inputs and have a 100 percent investment allowance on plant, machinery, equipment, and buildings. The Kenyan Export Processing Zones (EPZs) offer a variety of fiscal and in-kind incentives such as tax holidays, less red tape, administrative shortcuts, and superior infrastructure not found anywhere else in the country. Firms operating in EPZs are exempted from all withholding taxes on dividends and other payments to non-residents during the first 10 years. They are also exempted from import duties on machinery, raw materials, and intermediate inputs. There are no restrictions on management or technical arrangements, and EPZ companies have access to expedited licensing procedures. Kenya's EPZs have become the center of Kenya's successful garment and apparel sector.

EPZ firms are allowed to sell up to 20 percent of their output on the domestic market. However, they are liable for all taxes on products sold domestically plus a 2.5 percent penalty. There is no general system of preferential financing, although sectoral government development agencies in areas such as tourism and tea are supposed to provide funds at below-market rates to promote investment and exports. .

INTELLECTUAL PROPERTY RIGHTS (IPR) PROTECTION

Kenya is a member of most major international and regional intellectual property conventions including the World Intellectual Property Organization (WIPO), the African Regional Industrial Property Organization, the Paris Convention for the Protection of Industrial Property, and the Berne Convention on the Protection of Literary and Artistic Works. The Kenya Industrial Property Act (as amended) is the implementing legislation for Kenya's obligations under the WTO Trade-Related Aspects of Intellectual Property Rights (TRIPS) Agreement. U.S. industry has called on the Kenyan government to take a more active role in enforcing intellectual property protection and combating the spread of counterfeit and pirated goods. Pirated and counterfeit products in Kenya, mostly from South Asia and East Asia, present a major impediment to U.S. business interests in the country. Industry estimates that copyright piracy of business software, records, and music in Kenya cost U.S. firms $25 million in lost sales in 2005.

Patents and Trademarks

Patent protections are enshrined in Kenya's Trademarks Act, which established the Kenya Industrial Property Institute (KIPI). KIPI considers applications for and grants industrial property rights and privileges that are valid for 10 years on a renewable basis. The Amendments to the Act -- designed to bring Kenya into conformity with the Madrid Agreement and Protocol as well as the TRIPS Agreement -were passed and came into force in 2004. The act provides protection for registered trade and service marks and entitles foreign investors to national treatment and priority right recognition for their patents' and trademarks' filing dates.

Copyrights

Computer programs, sound recordings, broadcasts, and literary, musical, artistic, and audiovisual works are protected under the Copyright Act. The Kenya Copyright Board (KCB) is charged with coordinating all licensing and treaty activity and has the authority to inspect, seize, and detain suspect articles and to prosecute offenses. In June 2006, the Attorney General appointed the first KCB executive director. The KCB established an IPR enforcement unit in October 2006. The KCB has minimal staff and has not, to date, effectively carried out its mandate. Infringement of copyright, especially on music and films, is pervasive, and enforcement remains sporadic at best.

Kenyan artists have formed organizations to raise awareness of intellectual property rights and to lobby the government for better enforcement, but merchants are still free to peddle pirated versions of Kenyan and international works without fear of arrest or prosecution. Pirated materials and counterfeit goods produced in other countries are readily available in all major towns. These materials include pre-recorded audiocassette tapes, DVDs, CDs, and consumer products. General understanding of the importance of intellectual property is limited. In October 2005, however, the High Court ruled in favor of the plaintiff in a copyright infringement case (Alternative Media Limited vs. Safaricom Limited). In November 2006, the American Chamber of Commerce of Kenya, in conjunction with the Ministry of Trade and Industry and the Kenya Association of Manufacturers, held a pioneering regional IPR conference in Nairobi.

Enforcement

In July 2006, the Ministry of Trade and Industry reported that Kenyan manufacturers incur a net loss of Ksh30 billion (over $400 million) due to counterfeit products, while the government loses Ksh6 billion (approximately $80 million) in potential tax revenue annually due to counterfeit products. Imported drugs, shoes, textile products, office supplies, tubes and tires, batteries, shoe polish, soaps, and detergents are the most commonly counterfeited items. Historically, penalties and enforcement for copyright infringement have been low. The Attorney General has yet to introduce before Parliament a proposed Counterfeit Goods Bill that would strengthen the ability of law enforcement agencies to investigate and prosecute manufacturers and distributors of counterfeit and pirated goods. In December 2006, the

Minister of Trade and Industry presided over the destruction of 3.2 million counterfeit Bic pens that the Kenya Revenue Authority had confiscated.

SERVICES BARRIERS

In general, individuals and companies supplying services, whether local or foreign, are accorded the same treatment.

Telecommunications

Kenyan telecommunications are dominated by three state bodies: Telkom Kenya, the monopoly fixed-line services provider; the Communications Commission of Kenya (CCK), the regulatory body; and the Postal Corporation of Kenya. Kenya has witnessed significant growth in the information, communication, and technology sector in terms of telephones lines, Internet Service Providers (ISPs), and the number of Internet users and broadcasting stations.

The government has liberalized the mobile telephone market. In January 2005, the government ended Telkom Kenya's monopoly on Very Small Aperture Terminals (VSATs) and Internet bandwidth, and subsequently licensed a number of competing firms. In August 2005, CCK issued guidelines on the provision of Voice-Over-Internet Protocol (VoIP) and to date there are a number of licensed VoIP providers operating in the country.

In February 2006, the CCK de-registered 30 Internet Service Providers (ISPs). By June 2006, there were 53 registered ISPs in operation, 19 public data network operators, and six commercial VSAT hub operators. There were also two licensed call centers, but only one was in operation. Foreign ownership of an ISP is restricted to 40 percent.

Since 2004, Kenya's updated regulatory framework includes:

- Permitting mobile operators (GSM) to construct and operate their own international gateways;
- Issuing additional licenses to provide Internet backbone and gateway, broadcast signal distribution, and commercial VSAT services on a first-come, first-served basis;
- Allowing public data network operators (PDNOs) to establish international gateways for data communication services; and
- Allowing Internet backbone and gateway operators, broadcast signal distributors, commercial VSAT operators, and public data network operators to carry any form of multimedia traffic.

In a new National Information and Communication Technology Policy released in late 2005, the government proposed major changes in the sector, including a further restructuring of Telkom Kenya. The telecommunications parastatal's privatization is now scheduled for April 2007.

In September 2006, the government announced the results of a pre-qualification exercise for a second national operator (SNO) for fixed-line telephone services in which seven firms/consortia were selected. In late October 2006, the press announced that CCK had offered the SNO license to operate both fixed and mobile telephone services to a Dubai-based company. However, the deal fell apart and the second-highest bidder, an Indian company, was offered the license and, reportedly, has accepted.

In September 2006, a Kenyan court ruling ended an ownership dispute that had prevented Econet Wireless from exercising its rights to roll out a new mobile network under a license it had won in 2004. As of the end of 2006, however, the CCK still had not provided the company with the network codes necessary to begin its roll-out, and the company publicly accused government officials of corruption in the matter.

To date, the deficiency of competition has contributed to increased costs of doing business. Consumers complain that Telkom Kenya's land lines are often down and that cell phone service is too expensive. Like the fixed-line market, cellular service provides consumers with few options. Currently only two mobile phone firms, Safaricom (a joint venture of Telkom Kenya and Vodafone) and Celtel (a joint venture of Vivendi and Sameer Investments), are licensed to provide mobile telecommunications. As of June 2006, Safaricom and Celtel had over 6.5 million subscribers, up from 4.6 million from June 2005. Safaricom commands over 66 percent of the market share. The government intends to sell 34 percent of the Safaricom shares it holds through Telkom Kenya through an initial public offer (IPO) on the Nairobi Stock Exchange while selling 26 percent to a strategic investor. In the current arrangement, 9 percent of the Safaricom shareholding will be sold to finance the sale of Telkom Kenya. Under the existing shareholders' agreement signed in 1999, the government cannot sell its shares of Vodafone, which has pre-emptive rights over the shares.

INVESTMENT BARRIERS

Kenya revised its investment promotion laws in late 2005. Foreign investors who seek to benefit from incentive programs under the Investment Promotion Act of 2004, as amended, must obtain a certificate from the newly established Kenya Investment Authority and confirm that the amount to be invested is equivalent to at least $100,000. Domestic investors are required to invest a minimum of Ksh5 million (approximately $70,000) to qualify. The Investment Promotion Act, as amended, reduces the number of required licenses from 71 to 18. The holder of an investment certificate immediately qualifies for all the required licenses listed in the Second Schedule of the Act. For a maximum period of 12 months after the issuance of an investment certificate, the licenses are deemed to have been issued, subject to the submission of appropriate forms and fees. According to the Ministry of Trade and Industry, with the establishment of the Kenya Investment Authority, the registration of foreign firms now involves a simple five-step process.

A Foreign Investment Advisory Service (FIAS) report found that many regulatory systems are outdated, do not serve an identifiable purpose, and are exploited by low-level officials to extract bribes. The report also found that the current business registration system in Kenya is archaic, inefficient and unreliable. Starting a business takes on average over 54 days, lower than the regional average of 61.8 days but significantly higher than EAC neighbors Uganda and Tanzania (30 days). A private sector initiative found that the government maintained 1,300 license and fee requirements that have a direct or indirect impact on trade and investment. However, in June 2006, the government abolished 37 licenses and appointed a commission to eliminate or simplify an additional 700 licenses that directly affect trade and investment in the country. Reviews of the legal sector found that the court system is in disarray, with a huge and growing backlog of cases. Corruption and inefficiency further reduce the credibility of the legal and judicial systems in Kenya. These deficiencies continue to be an obstacle to investment, especially since they make financial institutions reluctant to make loans and increase the risk premium.

The Kenyan government allows up to 75 percent foreign ownership (personal or corporate) of firms listed on the Nairobi Stock Exchange (NSE). If foreign ownership in a company is 75 percent at the time of listing on the NSE, the foreign owner is allowed to maintain (or reduce) but not to increase its share. Foreign investors may be allowed to increase their investment with prior written approval from the Capital Market Authority if the shares reserved for local investors are not fully subscribed. Foreign brokerage companies and fund management firms must be locally registered companies, with Kenyan ownership of at least 30 percent and 51 percent, respectively. Foreign ownership of equity in insurance, telecommunications, and companies listed on the Nairobi Stock Exchange is restricted to 66.7 percent, 70 percent, and 75 percent respectively. Foreign equity in companies engaged in fishing activities is restricted to 49 percent of the voting shares as stipulated by the Fisheries Act of 1991.

Foreigners are not permitted to hold a freehold land title anywhere in the country, but can be granted leasehold titles -- normally 99 years for land in towns and coastal beachfronts, and 999 years elsewhere. Investors in Kenya are required to comply with environmental standards that are enforced through the licensing regime. The cumbersome and opaque process required to purchase land, and concerns about security of title because of past abuses relating to distribution of public land, constitute serious impediments to new investment. An investment guide to Kenya, published by the United Nations and International Chamber of Commerce in June 2005, asserts that individuals and companies involved in business disputes routinely turn to the courts for redress of grievances. Although arbitration and alternative dispute resolution are becoming increasingly popular, most disputes are still resolved through litigation in the courts. Lack of confidence in the speedy and fair resolution of disputes, and requests from officials for illicit payments, continue to dampen the country's ability to attract more foreign investment.

Kenya has been slow to open public infrastructure to competition because the state-owned companies that control infrastructure are considered "strategic" enterprises. The reform and partial privatization of the telecommunications, power, and rail sectors has fallen behind schedule, but is proceeding. The Kenyan Parliament passed a Privatization Law in 2005 that outlines how the government will divest its shares in the state corporations. In May 2006, the government-owned Kenya Electricity Company sold 30 percent of its shares. The Mumias Sugar Company and Kenya Commercial Bank, among other entities previously considered "strategic parastatals," are lined up for privatization in the coming year. In November 2006, the Kenyan and Ugandan governments entered into a 25-year concession agreement with "Rift Valley Railways," a consortium led by a South African firm to run the Kenya-Uganda railroad. The Kenya Port Authority plans to privatize some of its functions in the Port of Mombasa.

Kenya applies fees and security bonds in an attempt to discourage the employment of foreign labor. New foreign investors with expatriate staff are required to submit plans for the gradual phasing out of non-Kenyan employees. Some investors continue to complain that it is difficult to obtain work permits for expatriate staff.

OTHER BARRIERS

Customs Clearance

Recent changes by the Kenya Revenue Authority for electronic customs clearances have created some confusion and delays at Kenya's ports of entry. Until the program is improved, revised, or eliminated in favor of port of entry inspections, it will pose an added expense and administrative burden on exporters to Kenya. Also, allegations of corruption and on-going delays in cargo handling at the Port of Mombasa, the region's major trade hub, continue to add unnecessary costs for exporters. In response to demands from Kenyan exporters and the Kenya Association of Manufacturers (KAM), in October 2006 the government vowed to begin 24-hour, round-the-clock customs services at the port, but is still working out the operational and budget details.

Corruption

Corruption remains a major deterrent to greater investment, both foreign and domestic, and government officials bemoaned the lack of foreign direct investment in 2005-2006. Transparency International's 2005 Corruption Perceptions Index places Kenya 145th among 159 countries surveyed. According to the International Finance Corporation's Investment Climate Assessment for Kenya, corruption was rated as a severe or major obstacle by three-quarters of firms surveyed, with two-thirds of respondents stating they were expected to pay bribes for government contracts. In late 2005 and early 2006 there were public disclosures of high-level, grand-scale graft in both the previous and current administrations. Calls for greater accountability on the part of the media, civil society, and donors led to the unprecedented resignation of three cabinet ministers in early 2006, generating hopes that such activities may at last be on the wane. The Kenya Anti-Corruption Commission launched several investigations in 2006 against senior government officials. However, none of these cases has been successfully prosecuted, in large part due to bottlenecks in the Attorney General's Office and loopholes in the judiciary.

Chapter 3

NORWAY

TRADE SUMMARY

The U.S. goods trade deficit with Norway was $4.7 billion in 2006, a decrease of $152 million from $4.8 billion in 2005. U.S. goods exports in 2006 were $2.4 billion, up 23.3 percent from the previous year. Corresponding U.S. imports from Norway were $7.1 billion, up 4.5 percent. Norway is currently the 47th largest export market for U.S. goods.

U.S. exports of private commercial services (i.e., excluding military and government) to Norway were $2.1 billion in 2005 (latest data available), and U.S. imports were $2.0 billion. Sales of services in Norway by majority U.S.-owned affiliates were $3.4 billion in 2004 (latest data available), while sales of services in the United States by majority Norway-owned firms were $459 million.

The stock of U.S. foreign direct investment (FDI) in Norway in 2005 was $8.8 billion (latest data available), up from $8.4 billion in 2004. U.S. FDI in Norway is concentrated largely in the mining and manufacturing sectors.

IMPORT POLICIES

Industrial Goods

Norway, along with Switzerland, Iceland and Liechtenstein, is a member of the European Free Trade Association (EFTA). EFTA members, with the exception of Switzerland, participate in the European Union (EU) single market through the European Economic Area (EEA) accord. Norway grants preferential tariff rates to EEA members. As an EEA signatory, Norway assumes most of the rights and obligations of EU member states. The principal exception is in the agricultural sector, which the EEA accord does not cover.

Although Norway maintains a liberal trade and investment regime with respect to industrial products, its agricultural sector remains highly protected. Some of Norway's trade restrictions are more severe than those of the EU, such as non-tariff barriers related to approval for agricultural products derived from biotechnology. As a general matter, Norway has implemented or is in the process of implementing most EU trade policies and regulations. Therefore, U.S. exports to Norway face many of the same trade and investment barriers that limit U.S. access to the EU, such as the ban on hormone-treated meat products. As a non-EU member, Norway's ability to influence EU decisions is limited.

Norway's market, except for agricultural products and processed foods, is generally transparent and open. Norway has continued on a unilateral basis to dismantle import tariffs on industrial products. The average most favored nation (MFN) tariff on non-agricultural products has fallen from 2.3 percent in 2000 to less than 1 percent today. More than 90 percent of industrial tariff lines are currently duty-free.

Agricultural Products

Although agriculture accounts only for about 1 percent of Gross Domestic Product (GDP), Norway maintains strict protections that shelter the sector from global competition. As justification for this policy, Norway emphasizes the importance of "non-trade concerns," which include food security, environmental protection, rural employment and the maintenance of human settlement in sparsely populated areas.

One of Norway's leading concerns in the stalled WTO Doha Development Round has been the preservation of its highly subsidized and protected agricultural sector. Norway remains committed to advocating tariff, sensitive product and special product protections for its agricultural sector.

Agricultural Tariffs

Norway bound its tariffs for agricultural commodities in 1995 as part of its WTO commitments. Tariffication of agricultural non-tariff barriers as a result of the Uruguay Round led to the replacement of quotas with high *ad valorem* product tariffs. Although Norway is only 50 percent self-sufficient in agricultural production, it maintains a protective system that assures that domestic producers – farmers and the food processing industry – have little competition until all domestic production has been consumed. Tariff rates on agricultural products currently average about 38 percent – in comparison to less than 1 percent for non-agricultural products – and can range as high as several hundred percent.

Domestic agricultural shortages and price surges have been offset by temporary tariff reductions. Lack of predictability in tariff adjustments and insufficient advance notifications – generally only two to five days before implementation – favor nearby European suppliers and make imports from the United States, especially of fruit, vegetables and other perishable horticultural products, very difficult. For a number of processed food products, tariffs are applied based on their recipes, requiring the Norwegian importer to provide a detailed disclosure of product contents. Many exporters to the Norwegian market refuse to give all requested details and their products are, as a result, subjected to maximum tariffs.

Agricultural Tariff-Rate Quotas

Norwegian tariff-rate quotas are divided into two categories – minimum access quotas and Generalized System of Preferences (GSP) quotas. Tariff-rate quotas exist for grains and a number of horticultural products. In 2001, Norway also implemented auction quotas for grain and other carbohydrate feed. All quotas are traded at auctions held by the Norwegian Agricultural Authority, a Ministry of Agriculture agency that controls all agricultural imports.

Interest in the quotas among Norwegian importers is limited, except for grain, despite the substantial reductions in duties for some products. Compared with domestic consumption and production, the quotas are very small. Most of the interest in Norway's quota auction comes from smaller importers who use their quotas for niche products or from large farmer-owned companies to block competition to their own domestically-produced products.

Auction participation is inexpensive, and those who secure a quota are not required to actually import. Although about 98 percent of the quotas each year are sold on these auctions, only 30 percent to 40 percent of the quotas auctioned are usually filled through imports. There is no system to reallocate unused import quotas, hindering foreign exporters seeking access to the Norwegian market for these products.

Raw Material Price Compensation

Though Norway uses high import tariffs to protect domestic commodities from foreign competition, the situation is more complex for certain processed goods. Although the EEA does not generally apply to agricultural products, it includes provisions on raw material price compensation that are meant to increase trade in processed food. Norway has a special agreement with the EU within the EEA framework that grants some EU processed food products a preferential duty. In 2003, the agreement extended coverage to bread and baked goods, breakfast cereals, chocolate and sweets, ice cream, pasta, pizza, soups and sauces. This scheme disadvantages U.S. exporters in the Norwegian market for the covered processed foods.

Norway also maintains a price reduction scheme that includes subsidies for using certain domestically-produced raw materials in processed foods. Products for which such subsidies are paid include chocolate, sweets and ice cream (for milk and glucose), and pizza (for cheese and meat). The purpose of the system is to help compensate the domestic food processing industry for high domestic raw material costs.

EU-Based Agricultural Regulations

In addition to its own requirements related to the import of food products, Norway has generally implemented EU regulations since 1999. Some EU regulations that Norway has adopted inhibit trade, such as EU regulations on veterinary control of animals and animal products requiring that meat products entering the country come from an EU-approved plant and be accompanied by the necessary certificates. The importer in Norway must be registered and notify authorities in advance of the arrival of any shipment (24 hours in advance for plants and 30 days in advance for animals). Except for fish products, shipments must enter through either Oslo harbor or Oslo airport. Twenty entrance locations exist for fish products.

Norway also implements EU regulations that bar imports of meat from animals treated with growth hormones. However, the market for U.S. beef for consumption on cruise ships based in, or calling on, Norwegian ports is burgeoning, as beef consumed on board is not subject to such import restrictions.

Biotechnology

Norway's strict limitations on imports of agricultural biotechnology products have had an adverse impact on U.S. producers. Before the limitations took effect in 1996, U.S. exporters usually supplied 60 percent to 80 percent of the Norwegian soybean market. As a result of the limitations, the entire market has been lost.

Although not a member of the EU, as an EEA member, Norway is required to implement EU legislation with regard to food, feed and seed produced from genetic engineering. However, the Norwegian Gene Technology Act of 1993 is more restrictive than EU legislation as it requires proof that agricultural biotechnology products were developed with an ethical justification, provide a societal benefit and accord with sustainable development goals. In 2004, the EU implemented Regulation 1829/2003 on Genetically Modified Food and Feed, as well as Regulation 1830/2003 on Traceability and Labeling of Genetically Modified Organisms and the Traceability of Food and Feed Products produced from Genetically Modified Organisms. These polices were integrated into Norwegian regulations in September 2005.

While the revised Norwegian regulations incorporated the major elements of the EU regulations, they do not represent a formal or complete implementation of EU directives. All food and feed produced from genetic engineering, including products that no longer contain detectable traces of agricultural products derived from biotechnology, must be labeled. The allowable adventitious presence level is set at 0.9 percent for EU-approved products and 0.5 percent for products that have not yet been approved but have successfully completed an EU or Norwegian risk assessment. All products testing above these levels must be labeled. The regulation does not require labeling of products that are not food ingredients, such as processing aids. Meat, milk or eggs obtained from animals fed with products derived from biotechnology or treated with medicinal products derived from biotechnology do not require additional labeling.

Wines and Spirits

The wine and spirits retail market in Norway is controlled by the government monopoly Vinmonopolet. There were 198 Vinmonopolet stores throughout Norway at the end of 2006. Wine and spirits sales through ordinary retail stores are not allowed. An approved importer/agent and distributor are required in order to enter the market. Gaining approvals to include wines and other alcoholic beverages on Vinmonopolet's retail list is cumbersome, limiting the variety of U.S. wines available to Norwegian consumers. Vinmonopolet relies on a tender system, with set specifications and conditions for quality, price and delivery, in acquiring most new products. Products chosen for sale through Vinmonopolet must meet annual minimum sales quotas or they are dropped from the inventory. Advertising of alcoholic beverages is strictly prohibited.

GOVERNMENT PROCUREMENT

Norway is a signatory to the WTO Agreement on Government Procurement (GPA). Norway's government procurement procedures are non-discriminatory and based on open, competitive bidding for procurement above certain threshold values. A similar set of national rules applies to public contract tenders below these thresholds. Exceptions for defense procurement leave a "gray area" for items such as rescue helicopters that can also be used in military operations. Although disputes may be settled by the European Surveillance Authority (ESA) or by the courts, the process can be unduly lengthy.

INTELLECTUAL PROPERTY RIGHTS (IPR) PROTECTION

Internet piracy and cable/satellite decoder and smart card piracy have risen in Norway. Broadband Internet is standard, making peer-to-peer downloads of music and video easy and common. Encoding groups that release early copies of new motion pictures on the Internet are problematic. Television and cable companies are active in combating decoder and smart card piracy, and satellite operators recently introduced conditional access technologies that have mitigated the problem. Private organizations like the Motion Picture Association are attempting to raise public awareness of Internet and video piracy, for example, by running anti-pirating advertisements in movie theaters. Norwegian authorities have not undertaken any serious public relations efforts to combat Internet or other piracy of copyrighted property.

Copyright

In June 2005, Norway enacted legislation based on the EU's 2001 Copyright Directive that combats Internet piracy and addresses some gaps in Norway's IPR protections. The legislation bans unauthorized peer-to-peer file sharing and requires that creative works can be downloaded from the Internet only with the artist's prior approval. However, contrary to the EU Copyright Directive, Norway has failed to provide rights holders the ability to seek injunctive relief against Internet Service Providers who allow pirate websites to operate on their networks.

The legislation also grants legal protection to technological protection measures designed to prevent unauthorized use of a creative work. The law bars the intentional circumvention of such systems in most circumstances. However, an exception is made for "private use." Norway thus expressly allows circumvention of copy protection and other technical measures for private use of copyrighted materials other than computer software. For example, this measure allows music CD owners to breach protection measures in order to transfer copyrighted music. Although not expressly stated in the law, the legislative history of this provision suggests that "private use" also includes providing free copies to family and friends. In compensation, Norway budgeted NOK32.5 million ($5 million) in 2005 and NOK33.5 million in 2006 for payments to adversely affected music and motion picture rights holders. Norway plans to make such payments annually from future government budgets. However, the funds will be paid only to artists in the EU and EFTA countries, though copyrighted U.S.

products undoubtedly comprise a high percentage of downloaded material. The funds are distributed by a non-governmental organization, the Norwegian Organization of Rightholders in Audio-visual Works (NORWACO), which uses radio air time statistics to determine their allocation among EU/EFTA artists.

The EFTA Surveillance Authority is reviewing whether Norway has correctly implemented the EU Copyright Directive.

Counterfeit and Pirated Goods

Norway does not expressly ban imports of counterfeit or pirated goods. A trademark or copyright holder must obtain a court order and have the case referred to the police before customs authorities will take action to stop entries of pirated goods. However, Norway's strict privacy laws bar customs authorities from informing rights holders when questionable shipments arrive at the border, rendering the remedy ineffective. Although counterfeit and pirated goods are not commonly available domestically, counterfeiters and intellectual property pirates use Norway as a "gateway" to third countries – importing illicit goods, paying applicable import duties and reshipping the goods to EU nations.

Enforcement

Enforcement of IPR protections is inconsistent. Norwegian police and judicial authorities are generally committed in principle to taking action against piracy and intellectual property right infringement, to the extent authorized by Norwegian law, and have successfully prosecuted a number of high-profile cases. However, the authorities lack the capability and resources to handle complaints about IPR violations effectively. Police authorities are aware of such problems as the "gateway" issue and have been working to address them, but with little result. Given limited resources, Norwegian law enforcement authorities have placed more priority on areas like computer crime than traditional IPR violations. For example, local business representatives indicate that complaints about copyright infringement usually either go unaddressed or are given low priority.

Digital Rights Management Technologies

In 2006, significant public attention developed in Norway with respect to the demands of some consumer advocates to mandate interoperability among consumer electronic devices used for downloading and playing recorded music. While it is not clear whether Norwegian law will be amended to address interoperability of digital rights management (DRM) technologies, this issue bears continued monitoring to ensure that the intellectual property rights of DRM developers and of artists whose copyrighted works are protected by DRM technologies remain fully respected.

SERVICES BARRIERS

Financial Sector

Current regulations require that the Norwegian Financial Supervisory Authority grant permission for ownership levels in local financial institutions that exceed certain thresholds. The Authority assesses the acquisitions to ensure that prospective buyers are financially stable and the acquisition does not unduly limit competition. The Authority applies national treatment to non-bank foreign financial groups and institutions, but applies nationality restrictions to bank ownership. At least half the members of the board and half the members of the corporate assembly of a financial institution must be nationals and permanent residents of Norway or another EEA nation. On January 1, 2005, Norway removed the ceiling on foreign equity in a Norwegian financial institution, provided the Authority has granted a concession. Norway grants branches of U.S. and other foreign financial institutions the same treatment as domestic institutions.

Telecommunications Sector

In 1998, Norway began to liberalize the telecommunications services sector. The former monopoly provider – Telenor – was partially privatized in December 2000, leaving the government with a stake of 78 percent. Since that time, the government's share has declined to about 54 percent, though Norway's new government has indicated it will suspend further privatization of state-controlled companies.

Telenor remains the dominant operator in the Norwegian telecommunications market. In 2005, the Norwegian Post and Telecommunications Authority (NPTA), in line with the EU's telecommunications regulatory framework, declared that Telenor had significant market power in a number of segments in the telecommunications sector including: leased lines; call origination; transit services; wholesale unbundled access to metallic loops and sub-loops for the purpose of providing broadband and voice services; wholesale broadband access; and wholesale transmission services for national radio, local television and national television on analogue terrestrial networks. New regulatory obligations have been imposed on Telenor by the NPTA in order to facilitate competitors' entry into and further access to these markets.

The introduction of Voice-over Internet Protocol (VoIP) telephone services has further encouraged competition among telecommunications operators in Norway. The NPTA released an outline of regulation on VoIP services in April 2005.

INVESTMENT BARRIERS

Norway welcomes foreign investment as a matter of policy and grants national treatment to foreign investors, except in financial services, mining, hydropower and property acquisition. Foreign companies are required to obtain concessions for the right to own or use various kinds of real property, including forests, mines, tilled land and waterfalls. However, foreign companies do not need concessions to rent real estate, provided that the rental contract is made for a period of fewer than ten years.

In the offshore petroleum sector, Norwegian authorities encourage – but do not require – the use of Norwegian goods and services. The Norwegian share of the total supply of goods and services in this sector has remained high (approximately 50 percent) over the last decade. Norway's petroleum concession process still operates on a discretionary basis, with the government awarding licenses based on subjective factors rather than competitive bidding. Though the Norwegian government has in the past shown a strong preference for Norwegian petroleum companies in awarding the most promising oil and gas exploration and development blocks, foreign companies report no discrimination on the basis of nationality in recent licensing rounds. Norway has implemented EU directives requiring equal treatment of EEA oil and gas companies.

The Norwegian government maintains monopolies for certain postal services (letters under 50 grams), railways and the retail sale of alcohol. The government rarely allows foreign investment in hydropower production, and such investments, if approved, are limited to 20 percent equity participation. Norway has fully opened the electricity distribution system to foreign participation.

State Ownership and Control of Commercial Enterprises

The government continues to play a strong role in the Norwegian economy through its ownership and/or control of many of the country's leading commercial firms. The public sector accounts for nearly 60 percent of Norway's GDP. Central or local authorities own approximately 35 percent of the companies listed on the Oslo Stock Exchange, and more than one-third of the stock exchange's capitalization is in government hands.

A 2002 government "White Paper" called for reducing and improving state ownership in the economy. Norway took steps over the last several years to implement that policy, partially privatizing some of the country's leading firms (e.g., Statoil, Norsk Hydro, Telenor and others). However, the government coalition that took office in fall 2005 has halted further privatization of state-controlled companies.

Government Pension Fund

In 2004, the Norwegian Ministry of Finance adopted ethical guidelines for the "Government Pension Fund - Global" (the Fund). The Fund is composed of 78 percent tax revenue the government of Norway receives from petroleum profits and from returns on its direct interests in petroleum production licenses; this capital is then invested entirely in foreign financial instruments. At the end of 2006, assets accumulated in the Fund stood at more than $270 billion. The ethical guidelines state that the Norwegian Central Bank, which manages the Fund, may exclude investments in, or divest itself from, companies that: (1) produce weapons, such as nuclear arms or cluster bombs, that may violate humanitarian principles; or (2) contribute to serious violations of fundamental ethical norms, such as through human rights violations, severe environmental damage or gross corruption. In 2006, the Finance Ministry, on the recommendation of the Fund's Council on Ethics, instructed the

Central Bank to divest shares in a number of companies, the majority of which are from the United States. The U.S. Government has urged Norway to work toward greater transparency and more formal procedural structures for the Fund's decision-making.

OTHER SECTORAL POLICIES

Pharmaceuticals

Foreign pharmaceutical firms continue to experience difficulties in the Norwegian market. Until 1992, Norway limited patent protection for pharmaceuticals to the manufacturing process for a drug's active ingredient. Although Norway introduced product patents for pharmaceuticals in 1992, the previous system has left a difficult legacy for pharmaceutical companies as competitors claiming to use non-patented processes have recently entered the market. Several U.S. pharmaceutical companies are involved in legal actions in Norwegian courts alleging infringement by these new entrants. One U.S. company lost a preliminary injunction in a patent infringement case in 2006, which allowed the copycat drug to enter the market immediately, cost the company significant revenue, and led to layoffs of local employees. In 2006, affected multinational pharmaceutical companies, supported by the U.S. and two European embassies, advocated that Norway amend the public health care system's drug reimbursement regulations to bar pharmacies from substituting generics for branded drugs that have process patents. The Norwegian government rejected the appeals in June 2006.

Transparency on pricing, reimbursement decisions and recommendations is lacking. U.S. pharmaceutical products often face lengthy delays in securing approval for their products' inclusion in the state health care reimbursement scheme. Reimbursement and approval decisions are complex and political, with the Parliament making final decisions as part of its budget process.

The Norwegian Medicines Agency (NMA) added another potential hurdle to reimbursement approvals in 2005 by denying a U.S. pharmaceutical manufacturer's reimbursement application for lack of documentary proof – which would have taken several years to develop – that the costs of the drug in question compared reasonably with its treatment value and the costs of alternative treatments. The NMA's procedures for reviewing reimbursement applications neither require such cost-benefit data nor make them a factor in reimbursement decisions. The drug at issue is reimbursed in all EU countries except Denmark, and no other EU country requested such data as a condition of approving reimbursement. Requiring manufacturers to perform multi-year cost benefit studies of medically approved pharmaceuticals as a condition of reimbursement will result in significant additional costs and delays in bringing new drugs to the Norwegian market.

U.S. pharmaceutical manufacturers cite Norway's total prohibition of supplying product information to consumers – ranging from advertising to scientific data – as a barrier to market entry and expansion. Consumers are not fully informed about pharmaceutical innovations, sometimes delaying consumer access to the latest medicines.

The Norwegian Association of Pharmaceutical Manufacturers, which includes U.S. pharmaceutical firms, has complained about Norway's inadequate implementation of EU directives on transparency of measures regulating medicinal products for human use. Although Norway complies with the letter of EU requirements that reimbursement applications be acted on within 180 days, Norwegian authorities often reject applications as the period expires, giving them an unlimited amount of time to consider applications once appealed.

Automotive Sector

The general vehicle taxation system that Norway put into place in 1996, under which taxes are calculated progressively on the basis of vehicle weight, engine horsepower, and engine displacement, has had a strong negative impact on sales of U.S. vehicles in Norway. These parameters tend to be unfavorable to vehicles manufactured in the United States, which are generally heavier and equipped with engines with more horsepower and higher displacement than vehicles manufactured in other nations. In the year before this tax regime went into effect, approximately 9,500 American vehicles were sold in Norway, nearly 8 percent of the market. Since that time, sales of U.S. vehicles in Norway have steadily declined, to less than 1,500 in 2005 (about 1 percent of the market), most of which were light trucks. However, in its 2006 budget, the Norwegian government imposed new taxes on light trucks that, in effect, eliminated the last significant remaining market for U.S. vehicles in Norway. More than 1,000 U.S. light trucks were sold in Norway before the tax went into effect. Post-tax sales plummeted to several dozen vehicles.

Norway announced in October 2006 that it would substitute a new CO_2 emissions factor for the engine displacement parameter in its vehicle taxation regime, effective January 1, 2007. The new system is expected to encourage sales of diesel-powered passenger vehicles, which generally are not manufactured in the United States. Moreover, Norway will accept only European standards for measuring CO_2 emissions, further disadvantaging vehicles manufactured in the United States. Norway announced that it would lift the light truck tax in 2007 for trucks with cargo space above certain limits, but the space limitations deny most U.S. light trucks the benefit of the restored exemption.

Chapter 4

RUSSIA

TRADE SUMMARY

The U.S. goods trade deficit with Russia was $15.1 billion in 2006, an increase of $3.7 billion from $11.3 billion in 2005. U.S. goods exports in 2006 were $4.7 billion, up 19.1 percent from the previous year. Corresponding U.S. imports from Russia were $19.8 billion, up 29.3 percent. Russia is currently the 33rd largest export market for U.S. goods.

The stock of U.S. foreign direct investment (FDI) in Russia in 2005 was $5.5 billion (latest data available), up from $3.8 billion in 2004. This number does not yet reflect substantial U.S. investments in Russia during 2006 in the energy, automotive, food-processing, consumer goods, information technology and banking sectors.

Russia is in the process of negotiating terms of accession to the World Trade Organization (WTO). On November 19, 2006, the United States and the Russian government signed a WTO bilateral market access agreement. The terms of that agreement are on USTR's website at :http://www.ustr.gov/World_Regions/Europe_Middle_East/ Russia_the_NIS/ Section_Index.html. The Russian government has completed its bilateral market access negotiations with most other interested WTO Members, and is now focused on multilateral negotiations regarding its terms for accession, as well as completing its implementation of WTO provisions, from the rules agreements covering areas such as non-tariff barriers and intellectual property rights to ensuring that state-owned and state-trading enterprises operate solely on commercial terms when they are engaged in commercial activity. To enter the WTO, the Russian government must also complete negotiations with WTO Members on the levels of funding for certain programs supporting its agriculture sector.

IMPORT POLICIES

Russia continues to maintain a number of barriers with respect to imports, including tariffs and tariff-rate quotas, charges and fees, and licensing, registration and certification regimes. Discussions continue within the context of Russia's WTO accession to eliminate these measures or modify them so that they are consistent with internationally accepted practices.

Quotas

In January 2003, the Russian government announced the imposition of a quota for poultry and tariff-rate quotas (TRQs) for pork and beef. These quotas became effective in April 2003 and May 2003, respectively. A United States – Russia Bilateral Meat Agreement (Meat Agreement) was signed in June 2005, establishing TRQs for beef, poultry, and pork, and a 15 percent tariff for U.S. high quality beef. It also calls for bilateral negotiations in 2009 to determine whether the TRQs will remain or whether Russia will provide tariff-only treatment for these products. Quota allocations under the Meat Agreement are based on historical export levels. The United States was actively engaged with the Russian government throughout 2006 to ensure that U.S. producers of poultry, pork, and beef continued to have access to the Russian market and that Russia implemented its obligations under the Meat Agreement. The WTO bilateral market access agreement with the United States sets out a framework, including the time schedule, for WTO negotiations on how such goods will be treated post-2009.

Import and Activity Licenses

Import licenses and activity licenses required for wholesale and manufacturing activities are necessary to import products such as alcoholic beverages, pharmaceuticals, products containing encryption technology, explosive substances, drugs, nuclear substances, hazardous wastes, and some food products.

The 2005 Law on Spirits eliminated some licensing requirements and discriminatory fees applied to imported spirits, but it established the requirement that importers must register with the Ministry of Economic Development and Trade (MEDT) and obtain a general activity license from the Federal Tax Service, Ministry of Finance. The fee for obtaining the wholesale license, which is valid for five years and is subject to annual inspections, is approximately $9,500.

As part of the bilateral WTO market access agreement with the United States, the Russian government agreed to set up a streamlined system for the import of goods containing encryption technology with transparent, nondiscriminatory and WTO-consistent procedures. The Russian government also agreed to allow the importation of most commercially-traded information technology and telecommunications goods after a one-time notification, or in some cases, with no licensing or evaluation requirements at all. The U.S. Government will continue to work on addressing the licensing barriers to trade in goods containing encryption technology and other products subject to licensing requirements. The system will operate on an interim basis in 2007.

Customs Issues, Taxes and Tariffs

In addition to tariffs, there are two types of charges applied to imports: the Value Added Tax (VAT) and selective excise taxes. The universal VAT rate was reduced from 20 percent to 18 percent in 2004, with the exception of foodstuffs, pharmaceuticals and medical supplies, for which the VAT is 10 percent. Some medical equipment is totally exempted from the

VAT. Pharmaceutical importers have complained that new pharmaceuticals imported in the clinical trial stage (prior to registration) were improperly assessed the VAT because they could not produce a certificate of registration. There are ongoing discussions within the Russian government to lower the VAT further to 15 percent or 16 percent. However, no such proposals were included in the 2007 government budget law passed by Russia's parliament, the Duma.

The excise tax applies to a number of luxury goods, such as alcohol and cigarettes. Excise taxes for wine and spirits are 19.5 rubles per liter of ethyl alcohol and up to 108 rubles per liter for some wines. U.S. companies have faced significant obstacles trying to comply with the requirement to affix an excise stamp on bottles of spirits for which the excise tax has been paid (see Non-Tariff Barriers section). Excise taxes on other goods can total as much as 570 percent *ad valorem*.

U.S. industries complain of high tariffs on agricultural products such as sugar, distilled spirits, wine, fruit, processed food and forest products. As part of its WTO accession, Russia has agreed to bind its tariffs on all agricultural products, thereby providing more predictability on its tariff rates when Russia joins the WTO.

Russian import tariffs on automobiles, aircraft, and aircraft parts have presented particular obstacles to U.S. exports to Russia. The effect of the tariff, VAT and customs handling fees on aircraft was equivalent to a tax of 40 percent, making it virtually impossible for Russian airlines to afford to purchase foreign planes. The bilateral WTO market access agreement with the United States on tariffs and the bilateral agreement on leased aircraft will yield significant market access opportunities. When Russia joins the WTO, tariffs on aircraft will be substantially reduced. Tariffs on civil aircraft parts, including engines, will be reduced to an average of 5 percent. An agreement on leased aircraft, which entered into force on November 19, 2006, will immediately reduce tariffs on narrow body leased aircraft.

The current import duty on new passenger vehicles is 25 percent, to which an excise tax based on engine displacement and a VAT tax are added. The combination of these charges can increase import prices by 70 percent for larger U.S. passenger cars and sport utility vehicles. For motorcycles, Russia imposes a 20 percent special duty on large motorcycles, plus an additional 18 percent VAT, significantly increasing prices on imported large motorcycles.

In October 2006, Russia extended for 10 months an increase in the import duties to 15 percent on combine harvesters and threshers. Under the bilateral market access agreement on Russia's accession to the WTO, Russia agreed to rescind this increase by no later than July 2007, after which time duties will remain at 5 percent and will be bound upon accession.

As part of the bilateral market access agreement, tariffs on other key U.S. industrial exports will be cut substantially as well. Once Russia joins the WTO and the U.S. Congress grants Permanent Normal Trade Relations (PNTR) status to Russia, Russian tariffs on industrial products will be bound at an average of 8 percent, a reduction of approximately 36 percent from the rates applied in 2000.

A new Customs Code, intended to bring Russia's customs regime into compliance with WTO requirements, came into force in 2004. It simplified customs processes and established specific procedures for the application and payment of tariffs. Russia also amended its Customs Tariff Law to update its Customs Valuation practices in line with WTO provisions. However, significant problems remain. The Russian government issues unpublished recommendations on import valuations to customs posts to help to combat undervaluation of imports by importers. However, these recommendations can also be applied as reference prices for customs valuation or substituted for the invoice value of the imports, making the practice WTO inconsistent. Russia also has not fully implemented the WTO Customs Valuation Agreement in its laws, and must issue additional regulations to complete the process prior to its WTO accession. In addition, Russia's current customs clearance fees are not compatible with WTO obligations and will have to be revised. In terms of systemic concerns, U.S. exporters to Russia report that customs enforcement varies by region and port of entry and that frequent changes in regulations are unpredictable, adding to costs and delays at the border. Russia does not provide for the right to appeal customs decisions without penalty to a judicial authority, and, as in the case of the valuation recommendations, does not publish all laws, regulations, judicial decisions, and administrative rulings of general application to customs matters. The United States is working with Russia to make substantial improvements on these customs issues in the multilateral WTO Working Party process as part of its accession to the WTO.

Non-Tariff Barriers

U.S. companies continue to face a number of non-tariff trade barriers when exporting to Russia. Non-tariff barriers are a topic of detailed discussions in Russia's WTO negotiations.

Pharmaceuticals
Decisions by the Russian government regarding which pharmaceutical products to place on reimbursement lists for state-provided healthcare are having an adverse impact on U.S. exports to Russia.

U.S. industry reports that higher-priced imports, which are often safer and of a higher quality than locally-produced pharmaceuticals, are often absent from reimbursement lists and state purchases because the government focuses more on price concerns than on the quality and safety of the products.

Alcohol
As part of Law FZ 171, the "Law on Production and Turnover of Alcohol," which went into force in April 2006, all customs duties, excise taxes and the VAT on alcohol now must be paid in advance of application for customs stamps, using a bank guarantee and deposit. The new regulatory regime relies on an information management system (UFAIS) for importers to print Universal Product Code (UPC) data on a stamp. This system, comprising both hardware and software, is expensive to purchase, difficult to use and has failed thus far to fulfill its purpose to track alcohol from manufacture or import to the retail sales point. There is no way to stamp miniature, food service-sized bottles (the stamps are too big). Businesses have experienced difficulties in re-stamping product imported prior to the new law's introduction, and software glitches have caused importers' data to be corrupted, costing them time and money.

The logistical and administrative problems above created a situation in 2006 where companies that wanted to comply with the Law's stamping requirement could not comply. For much of 2006, the new stamps were not available and then the stamping machinery did not work. As a result a large volume of spirits was not re-stamped in time and had to be removed from retail shelves and relocated in warehouses in July 2006. Many bottles of spirits remain in wholesale warehouses because the appropriate legal provisions have not been established for wholesalers to apply for and obtain stamps. Approximately $60 million in U.S.-origin products for which the excise taxes and associated fees have already been paid remain in warehouses. Meanwhile, wholesalers are not legally allowed to apply the stamps on behalf of importers. Although in early 2007 the Russian government extended further the deadline for the bottles to remain in wholesale without facing confiscation or destruction, the underlying problems have not been addressed. The United States and other foreign governments are pressing the Russian government bilaterally and in the WTO multilateral process to find a long-term solution to these problems on an urgent basis.

The new requirements on spirits alcohol – information reporting requirements, usage of the UFAIS system, payment of the excise tax, application of the excise stamp, and import and licensing requirements – are also imposed on products such as perfumes, cosmetics, household cleaners and solvents containing more than 1.5 percent alcohol. The implementation of these rules in April 2006 severely disrupted trade. Such goods were eventually given a temporary extension from the application of the UFAIS reporting requirement, a significant burden for the small retailers of such goods, until December 31, 2006. At the end of 2006, the Duma amended the law to extend this temporary exemption until July 2007. In addition, it permanently exempted products in aerosol cans from the alcohol-related requirements. The United States is encouraging further amendment of the law to permanently exempt all non-food goods containing alcohol from the alcohol-related requirements above.

Development of Nuclear Power Generation

In October 2006, Prime Minister Fradkov signed a decree officially approving the Federal Targeted Program (FTP) on "Development of Russian nuclear power and industry complex for years 2007-2010 and further until 2015." The major goal is to accelerate the development of Russia's nuclear power industry. In accordance with the program, the total capacity of Russia's nuclear power plants (NPP) should reach more than 33 gigawatts (GW) by 2015. If FTP is successfully completed, Russia will have commissioned 10 new power units with a total capacity over 11 GW, and 10 additional power units will be in various phases of construction. The export arm of Russia's nuclear power sector, Atomstroyexport, is a significant competitor to U.S. companies. Furthermore, Russia's lack of a nuclear liability law to provide adequate legal protection for U.S. firms creates a prohibitive risk to U.S. suppliers of equipment, fuel and nuclear energy services to Russia.

EXPORT POLICIES

The subsidy-like effect of Russia's current domestic gas pricing policy is a key issue due to the potentially adverse impact this policy may have on certain U.S. industries. The price of gas for Russian industrial consumers is artificially low and, according to numerous reports, prices are well below the full cost of production. The downstream effects of this pricing policy are significant, because gas sells on Russia's domestic market for approximately $40-$45/tcm, while estimates of cost-recovery levels are at roughly $35-$40/tcm, with gas exported to Europe fluctuating between $230 and $350/tcm over the past year. The Russian government recently approved a plan to increase domestic prices to European levels by 2011. Over time, this should provide an incentive for producers to adopt more efficient production practices and greater energy efficiency. The gas sector and Gazprom, Russia's near-monopoly supplier, play a significant role in Russia's economy. The Russian government is proceeding slowly and cautiously with reform of the sector.

Russia maintains export duties on approximately 460 types of products. The Russian government intends to gradually eliminate such duties, except for products deemed as strategic, such as hydrocarbons and scrap metals, although it introduced such duties on lumber in early 2007. In May 1999, Russia imposed a 15 percent export duty on ferrous steel scrap, which remained in effect in 2006. These export duties create distortions in ferrous scrap trade, an important input to steel. However, Russia has agreed to reduce this duty rate to one-third of current levels within five years of acceding to the WTO. Russia also currently maintains a 10 percent export duty on copper cathode while no export duty is charged on copper wire rod. These two export duties together have created a market distortion, which is promoting vertical integration within the Russian copper industry: Russian copper wire rod producers can obtain favorable prices on copper cathode inputs, since Russian cathode producers cannot export their product for its fair market value. As a result, it is advantageous to export the higher value-added product (copper wire rod). As part of the bilateral WTO market access agreement, however, Russia has agreed to eliminate its export duty on copper cathode within four years of its accession to the WTO.

A variety of agricultural products are subject to export licensing and/or tariffs, such as some fish products, cereals, oilseeds and wood products. Russia was not permitted to export beluga caviar in 2006, but a limited quota was approved under the Convention on the International Trade in Endangered Species (CITES) for 2007. No export quota was approved for certain other types of Russia caviar.

STANDARDS, TESTING, LABELING AND CERTIFICATION

U.S. companies cite technical regulations and related product testing and certification requirements as major obstacles to U.S. exports of industrial goods to Russia. Russian authorities require product testing and certification as a key element of the product approval process. Opportunities for testing and certification performed by competent bodies outside Russia to be recognized by Russian authorities for purposes of demonstrating compliance to their regulations are limited, and some view procedures associated with Russia's approach to "supplier's declaration of conformity" as unnecessarily burdensome. Manufacturers of telecommunications equipment, oil and gas equipment, and construction materials and equipment, in particular, have reported serious difficulties in obtaining product approvals within Russia. The current classification and approval system for food supplement and dietetic products is costly and lengthy. Food and dietetic products that are legally sold in the United States and the European Union are subject to an expensive and lengthy certification process in Russia that takes between three and five months. Products are also subject to redundant technical reviews conducted by both the Nutrition Institute and Ministry of Health, which take between six and twelve months.

The United States continues to work with the Russian government to bring its product regulations and certification requirements into conformity with international standards and practices. The Russian government is attempting to put in place the necessary legal and administrative framework to establish transparent procedures for developing and applying standards, technical regulations, and conformity assessment procedures to accomplish this goal. The December 2002 "Law on Technical Regulation" provides a framework for the development of specific requirements for industrial goods, as well as sanitary and phytosanitary requirements for agricultural commodities, processed foods, and plants. In early 2007, the Duma began the process of amending this key framework law. It remains unclear what the final changes will be and how those changes will affect: 1) the scope of coverage of the law; 2) the legal procedures that will be used to develop technical regulations within Russia; and 3) how stakeholders will be able to participate in the development of technical regulations in Russia.

In 2006, the Russian government took a decision on fees for the certification of products and services and issued a decree on the list of the goods as subject to mandatory certifications. It also continued implementing a program to develop or amend some 84 technical regulations that began in 2004. While drafts of some technical regulations have made their way to the Duma for approval, many remain to be completed and approved.

The Russian government has required imported pharmaceutical products to complete a complex certification process, but has said that it would move to a system of self-certification for pharmaceutical products. At the end of 2006, the first details about this contemplated new approach became available. On December 20, 2006, a lengthy list was published of documents and their related approvals and measures that are needed for registration of pharmaceuticals. While industry and the U.S. Government are still analyzing the impact of the new requirements, they do not appear to be an improvement over the existing practice, and do not appear to constitute a true self-certification process.

Sanitary and phytosanitary (SPS) restrictions have had a major negative effect on U.S. trade, with products deemed as "sensitive" by Russia being blocked, seemingly without a scientific basis. In early 2006, in the context of U.S. bilateral negotiations on Russia's accession to the WTO, the Russian government issued a decree allowing the adoption of international standards, guidelines and recommendations, such as those set by internationally recognized bodies such as Codex Alimentarius and the Office of International Epizootics (OIE). These international standards, guidelines, and recommendations formed the basis for addressing specific SPS issues. At the same time that the United States and Russia concluded the bilateral WTO market access agreement, Russia and the United States signed bilateral agreements to address SPS issues related to: trade in frozen pork; the certification of pork and poultry facilities for exporting products to Russia; trade in beef and beef by-products; and trade in products of modern biotechnology. The details of these agreements are set out below.

Pork

Historically, Russia has only accepted freezing as mitigation for trichinae for U.S. frozen pork destined for further processing. Costly testing for trichinae was required for all U.S. pork imported for retail sale. Russia has now agreed to accept freezing as mitigation for trichinae for U.S. pork for retail sale as well as for further processing. As a result, imports from certified plants are now permitted when accompanied by the export certificate that was agreed between Russia's veterinary service and the U.S. Department of Agriculture's Food Safety and Inspection Services (FSIS). These commitments went into effect on November 19, 2006.

Inspection of Facilities Producing Pork and Poultry

Previously, Russian and U.S. officials jointly inspected all pork or poultry facilities that wanted to export product to Russia. This onerous process delayed exports from new plants or plants needing to remedy a deficiency found during the joint audit until a joint inspection occurred. U.S. exporters also noted concerns about the time it took Russian officials to provide formal approval for facilities after the inspection and to provide an updated list of approved facilities to its customs officials so trade could begin. The WTO bilateral market access agreement authorizes FSIS to certify new facilities and/or facilities needing to remedy a deficiency found in the annual joint audit by Russian and FSIS officials. The Russian government also agreed to specific time frames to respond to requests to list the facilities approved by FSIS and to a new process for annual joint audits.

Export of Beef and Beef by-Products

U.S. exports of beef and beef by-products to Russia have been restricted since a case of bovine spongiform encephalopathy (BSE) was discovered in the United States in 2003. Russia immediately banned all imports of beef and beef by-products from the United States, thereby closing the largest U.S. export market for frozen livers. Pursuant to the terms of the WTO bilateral market access agreement, the Russian government will immediately open its market to de-boned beef, bone-in beef and beef by-products from cattle under 30 months of age. Once the OIE takes a decision on the U.S. risk status with regard to BSE, the Russian government will permit U.S. exports based on that risk status. This decision would open Russia's market to U.S. beef of all ages (excluding specified risk materials that the OIE requires to be removed).

Products of Modern Biotechnology

U.S. suppliers of products of modern biotechnology have faced an unpredictable regulatory environment in Russia. For example, Russian officials halted product registrations and approvals in the area of feeds in 2004, initiated legislative reforms and began work on the development of a new permanent regulatory system for all products of modern biotechnology. In accordance with the WTO bilateral market access agreement with the United States, Russia will maintain an interim approval and registration system for products of modern biotechnology that is science-based, transparent, predictable, and consistent with the WTO Agreement on the Application of Sanitary and Phytosanitary Measures (WTO SPS Agreement). In addition, Russia will establish a permanent biosafety regulatory system for products of modern biotechnology that is science-based, transparent, predictable, and consistent with the WTO SPS Agreement. The United States will have an opportunity to comment on the interim and permanent approval and registration systems for these products, and Russian officials will take U.S. comments into account. Although Russia agreed to register products covered by all pending applications that have received a favorable science-based risk assessment by November 15, 2006, the U.S. Government is continuing to follow-up on the registration process to ensure that all pending applications are addressed. Russia and the United States agreed to hold annual consultations on the status of applications for re-registration of products whose registrations have expired during the year and to establish an ongoing bilateral consultative mechanism to discuss issues of regulatory development in the area of agricultural biotechnology. The United States also continues to work with the Russian government on the significant reservations that U.S. industry has expressed regarding Russia's food labeling policy, including the substance of draft legislation on that subject.

In addition to these specific issues, exporters of agricultural goods face systemic concerns related to the certification of agricultural products. Russian authorities require phytosanitary and/or veterinary certificates for nearly all agricultural and processed food products. Russian authorities require that producers seek certificates from their domestic regulatory authorities for some products for which Russia has not provided scientific evidence of an alleged risk. For example, Russia requires certificates for roasted coffee, which due to the nature of the processing process, does not present a pest risk (and therefore, the United States does not issue a phytosanitary certification for roasted coffee). Russian authorities also require a sanitary-epidemiological certificate or certificate of state registration for the importation of non-food items such as styrofoam cups and furniture.

Also related to biotechnology, a ban by Russia on all U.S. rice imports was imposed in late September 2006, citing the discovery of genetically modified rice seeds in shipments of U.S. long grain rice. . This calls into question whether Russia observed WTO requirements as the ban was imposed without prior notice or sufficient justification. Furthermore, the ban was imposed on both biotechnology and conventional varieties of rice. In December 2006, Russia also imposed a ban on all origins of rice noting a variety of sanitary and phytosanitary concerns. Since the bans were imposed, the United States has been working both bilaterally and multilaterally to resolve this issue.

GOVERNMENT PROCUREMENT

The Russian government spends over a third of its budget on procurement; it spent more than $30 billion in 2005 on government procurement (2006 figures are not yet available). A new law on government procurement, (federal law "On Placement of Orders for Delivery of Goods, Performances of Works and Provision of Services for State and Municipal Needs") entered into force on January 1, 2006. It regulates tenders on all government purchases over $8,000 (except for those made in commodity exchanges). To improve transparency in the procurement process, tenders must be advertised on agency websites as well as on a consolidated government procurement website. The new law eliminates some restrictions on the participation of foreign suppliers, although it permits exceptions for reasons of national security or defense.

INTELLECTUAL PROPERTY RIGHTS (IPR) PROTECTION

U.S. industry continues to be concerned about the IPR situation in Russia. U.S. copyright industries estimate they lost in excess of $1.9 billion in 2005 due to copyright piracy in Russia (business software $894 million; records and music - $475 million; motion pictures - $266 million; entertainment software - $224 million; and books - $42 million).

In 2006, Russia's optical disc production capacity continued to be far in excess of domestic demand, with pirated products apparently intended not only for domestic consumption, but also for export. The U.S. film industry estimates that more than 80 percent of all DVDs and approximately 66 percent of music CDs on the Russian market are pirated. However, legitimate DVD sales are on the rise, in part due to increased law enforcement action against pirates and a growing preference by the middle class for high quality products. Internet piracy continued to be a serious concern. Criminal investigations are ongoing against operators of the Russia-based download website www.allofmp3.com, which offers global distribution of pirated music and is the most notorious of several problem websites operating within Russia.

U.S. and multinational companies continue to report patent infringement and counterfeiting of trademarked goods as a problem, especially for consumer goods, wine, distilled spirits and pharmaceuticals. Several U.S. firms have experienced problems with trademark counterfeiting, with Russian enterprises attempting to appropriate well-known foreign trademarks not currently active in Russia, although rights holders have been moderately successful in countering these schemes through the Russian court system or with the Russian Federal Service for Intellectual Property, Patents and Trademarks (Rospatent). U.S. firms should proactively take steps to protect their intellectual property in Russia, including registering their trademarks with Rospatent.

The United States is working to ensure that Russia takes appropriate actions to protect intellectual property rights. On November 19, 2006, as part of the WTO bilateral agreement, the U.S. Government and the Russian government concluded an agreement that sets out a blueprint for actions that Russia will take to address piracy and counterfeiting and improve protection and enforcement of intellectual property rights, both stated priorities of the Russian government. As part of the agreement, the Russian government has committed to fight optical disc and Internet piracy, protect pharmaceutical test data, deter piracy and counterfeiting through criminal penalties, strengthen border enforcement, and bring Russian laws into compliance with WTO and international IPR norms. This binding agreement is an integral part of the bilateral WTO market access agreement between the United States and Russia, and Russia's implementation of the commitments on IPR will be essential to completing the final multilateral negotiations on the overall accession package. In addition, the United States is reviewing Russia's status as a beneficiary country under the U.S. Generalized System of Preferences (GSP) Program. Russia has also been on the Special 301 Priority Watch List since 1997.

The most significant legislative development in 2006 was the Duma's consideration and adoption of Part IV of the Civil Code, which will replace most of Russia's IPR legislation with a single code. The Code and implementing regulations to be developed over the next year will go into effect on January 1, 2008. While Russian government ministries and the Duma took steps to address some concerns of certain rights holders and the U.S. Government regarding the new legislation, Part IV still contains provisions that raise concerns regarding consistency with WTO and other international agreements. The Russian government has pledged to ensure that Part IV and other IPR measures will be fully consistent with the WTO Agreement on Trade-Related Aspects of Intellectual Property Rights (TRIPS) upon Russia's accession to the WTO.

In September 2006, amendments to the Law on Copyright and Related Rights came into effect, providing rights holders control over Internet distribution of their work.

Russia continues to deny national treatment for protection of geographical indications. As well, under Article 39.3 of the TRIPS Agreement, Russia must protect against unfair commercial use of undisclosed data submitted to government authorities to obtain marketing approval of pharmaceutical and agricultural chemical products. Russia currently does not provide such protection for pharmaceutical products. In late 2005, the Russian government proposed legislative changes to address these concerns. Unfortunately, these changes were not considered by the Duma in 2006. Russia committed in the November 2006 bilateral WTO agreement with the United States to work with the Duma to enact legislation to implement Article 39.3 of TRIPS by June 1, 2007.

Enforcement

Poor enforcement of IPR is a pervasive problem. The prosecution and adjudication of intellectual property cases remains sporadic and inadequate; there is a lack of transparency and a failure to impose deterrent penalties. Russia's customs administration also needs to significantly strengthen its enforcement efforts. Russian authorities initiated some enforcement actions in 2006, including raids on some optical disc production facilities and investigation of Internet sites. The November 2006 bilateral WTO agreement with the United States calls for specific actions to improve IPR enforcement.

Statistics provided by the Russian government indicate that Russian law enforcement has started to take action against pirate optical disk producers in the last few years. According to the Ministry of Internal Affairs and Rosokhrankultura, the agency responsible for implementing Russia's 2001 Licensing Law for optical media producers, raids during the first nine months of 2006 resulted in seven license suspensions and eight criminal prosecutions of plant operators. The Russian government committed in the November 2006 bilateral WTO agreement with the United States to strengthen the licensing regime for optical media plants. Necessary changes include denying new licenses to applicants known to have been engaged in piracy.

In the area of copyright infringement, 2,924 criminal cases were initiated in 2005. In 2006, 6,432 cases were initiated as of November 1. Russian authorities reported that 1,615 individuals were convicted of copyright offenses in the first nine months of 2006, as compared to 1,450 in the entire year of 2005. In trademark protection, whereas 545 criminal cases were initiated in 2005, over 500 were initiated in the first half of 2006. In 2005, 78 people were convicted of trademark offenses. In the first half of 2006, 95 were convicted. Finally, with regard to Internet piracy, Russian authorities claim to have initiated criminal cases against eight Internet sites distributing illegal software or counterfeit audiovisual products. Investigation and prosecution of the operators of the pirate website www.allofmp3.com are also ongoing, although progress is slow and their prospects are uncertain. Meanwhile, the site continues to operate.

Judicial System

While the Russian government has intensified the investigation and criminal prosecution of intellectual property rights infringers, cases often fail at the prosecution stage and few convictions for IPR violations ever result in prison sentences. Even where Russian law provides for serious penalties such as the destruction of counterfeit or pirated goods, products seized during enforcement actions often are not destroyed and consequently may return to the stream of commerce even if they are found to be illegal. In addition, production lines and equipment used for IP infringing activities are rarely seized, allowing pirates to continue their illegal activities either elsewhere or under a different corporate entity. In the vast majority of cases, alleged infringers receive small fines or suspended prison sentences. As part of the November 2006 bilateral WTO agreement with the United States, the Russian government made a commitment to take criminal actions against commercial scale piracy, with the objective of permanently closing down the production of optical media containing pirated and counterfeit material. It has also undertaken commitments to enact legislative amendments to provide broader authority to order the seizure and destruction of machinery and materials used in the production of infringing goods, and to make other improvements to the IPR legislative framework.

Russian administrative and judicial review bodies are beginning to become active in protecting IPR, and the number of police and judges with relevant expertise, though still small, is expanding. At the prosecutorial and judicial levels, many officials still do not consider IPR infringement a serious offense when compared to other crimes, although an increasing number of prosecutors are willing to file cases related to copyright infringements. On June 19, 2006, the Russian Supreme Court Plenum adopted a long-awaited resolution issuing guidelines on the application of civil IPR legislation on copyright and neighboring rights. In the November 2006 agreement, the Russian government agreed to propose to Russia's Supreme Court that it clarify practices relating to the imposition of penalties for IPR crimes, including imposition of penalties that take into account the high degree of public harm from IPR infringement and the objective of preventing future crimes.

U.S. investors generally consider the Russian court system ill-prepared to handle sophisticated patent cases. However, a specialized higher patent chamber has been established at Rospatent, which has brought greater expertise and efficiency to the adjudication of patent and trademark disputes.

SERVICES BARRIERS

Reforms in Russia's economy during the last decade allowed new service sectors to emerge and contributed to the further development of existing sectors. Services providers often operated without sufficient regulatory and institutional framework, yet, in recent years, Russia's legislation and regulations have begun to catch up with the market. Russia's services market is relatively open to U.S. service suppliers in areas such as professional services and distribution, but specific problems remain in particular areas. The ability to provide services to public utilities and certain energy-related services (see section on energy), remains limited. The process for an individual or a company to obtain a license to provide a service remains difficult.

As part of the bilateral WTO market access agreement with the United States, Russia has committed to liberalization in a broad range of service sectors. Once Russia is a WTO Member and has Permanent Normal Trade Relations status, U.S. firms will have further improved access to service sectors including banking and securities, insurance, telecommunications, audio-visual services, distribution, express delivery, energy services, environmental services and professional services.

Financial Services and Insurance

The 1996 federal law "On Banks and Banking Activity" permits foreign banks to establish subsidiaries in Russia. As part of its bilateral WTO accession agreement with the United States, Russia has agreed to allow 100 percent foreign ownership in the banking sector. It has also agreed to allow the cross-border supply of services, such as financial leasing, financial information and data processing, credit cards and other types of payments, and advisory services. Starting in January 1, 2008, foreign-invested companies will be allowed to provide asset management services to investors. With respect to permitting banks to establish branches in Russia from abroad, the Russian government has indicated it will return to consideration of this issue upon joining the OECD or in the next multilateral round of WTO negotiations, whichever comes first.

While foreign-source banking capital in Russia now accounts for between 12 percent to 15 percent of aggregate banking capital, the Russian government retains the prerogative to limit the foreign-sourced element of charter capital to 50 percent of the total charter capital. Calculation of the foreign-sourced element of the cap, however, is subject to several exclusions. If the ratio of foreign-sourced to total charter capital ever exceeds the 50 percent cap, Russia's regulators have the discretion to take only those actions specified in Russia's WTO commitments.

In the insurance sector, foreign insurance companies have been allowed to operate in Russia since 1999, but are subject to a 49 percent equity restriction. Foreign firms that were active in Russia when this requirement came into effect, however, were grandfathered and are not subject to the foreign equity limit. In January 2004, a law came into effect that, based on a 1994 Russia-EU treaty, effectively exempts EUbased insurance companies from the 49 percent foreign equity limitation. This exemption also applies to insurance companies based in the EU that have since been purchased by non-EU foreign companies. The 2004 law retains the requirement that chief executives and chief accountants of foreign insurers operating in Russia be Russian citizens.

Total foreign capital in the Russian insurance sector is currently limited to 25 percent. The Russian government has agreed to a significant level of market access and national treatment for foreign insurance companies upon its accession to the WTO. As part of its bilateral WTO market access agreement with the United States, Russia will allow foreign insurance companies to operate through subsidiaries, including 100 percent foreign-owned non-life insurance companies, upon its accession to the WTO. The government of Russia has also agreed to allow insurance branching from abroad at the end of a nine-year transition period. As in the banking sector, Russia will maintain the discretion to limit foreign-sourced charter capital in the insurance sector. Exclusions from the ratio and limits on actions that Russia's regulators can take also apply to the insurance sector.

Telecommunications

In the telecommunications sector, the 2004 Law on Communications was amended in July 2006 by the law "On Information, Information Technologies and Information Protection." The 2006 law's impact on competitive alternative (non-incumbent) telecommunications operators, many of which enjoy large foreign investment, has been substantial, since these companies now fall under tight government regulation. In particular, regulations on interconnection – the process by which alternative operators connect their networks to the Russian public telephone network – place interconnection contracts and fees under the regulatory authority of the Ministry for Information Technologies and Communications. Alternative operators fear that these fees will be raised to subsidize network upgrades of government-owned and ministry-controlled local and long distance operators.

Many in the telecommunications industry have been disappointed that the new law has not improved transparency in the licensing process, and have criticized the five- to ten-year license validity, which they argue do not allow them sufficient time to recoup their investment. The Federal Anti-Monopoly Service has challenged in court the manner in which the Ministry for Information Technologies and Communications issues licenses to Russian mobile phone operators. As a result, the Ministry has been ordered to issue licenses on a non-discriminatory basis for all operators, which may benefit companies with foreign investment.

The Federal Anti-Monopoly Service, in September 2006, also cited the three largest mobile phone operating companies as charging discriminatory rates to other operators. Two of the three companies subsequently revised their rate schedules, but the third, allegedly linked to the Ministry for Information Technologies and Communications, has resisted.

The State Radio Frequency Commission (under the Ministry for Information Technologies and Communications) intends to allocate radio frequencies in the 1935-1980 MHz, 2010-2025 MHz and 2125-2170 MHz bands for the development of mobile IMT-2000/UMTS standard networks in Russia. As of January 16, 2007, Russia's Federal Communications Agency (Rossvyaz) began accepting bids through February 26, 2007 for three 3G licenses, on frequencies formerly reserved for military or government use but now being opened for commercial use. The license fees have been set at 2.64 million rubles (roughly US$100,000), but criteria for the winning bidder(s) will include significant investment in network infrastructure development under certain deadlines and successful bidders will be required to begin offering commercial 3G services within two years of gaining their licenses. Potential opportunities for U.S. companies will most likely be as subcontract suppliers to the successful bidders. In 2006, the Federal Agency for Networks started granting WiMAX licenses in the 2.5-2.7 GHz range.

Certification of new products in the telecommunications industry takes an average of two months, down from four months a few years ago, but the process still suffers from a lack of transparency.

There are significant barriers in the provision of satellite telecommunications services in Russia. In particular, satellite regulation is not transparent. The legal requirements and administrative responsibilities associated with the provision of these services appear to be discriminatory, with the Russian government demonstrating a preference for Russian satellite communications systems, which puts competing satellite systems at a disadvantage.

The satellite industry reports that there is a burdensome certification process in place, and a local presence requirement further creates barriers to doing business in Russia.

Telecommunications and media services companies also report investment restrictions. Russian entities with more than 50 percent foreign ownership are prohibited from sponsoring television and video programs or from establishing television organizations capable of being received in more than 50 percent of Russia's territory or by more than 50 percent of the population.

INVESTMENT BARRIERS

Despite the passage of a law regulating foreign investment in June 1999, Russian foreign investment regulations and notification requirements can be confusing and contradictory. Corruption in commercial and bureaucratic transactions and problems with the implementation of customs regulations also inhibit investment. U.S. trade and investment in Russia would benefit from improved dispute resolution mechanisms, better protection of minority stockholder rights, the adoption of international accounting standards, and the adherence by companies to business codes of conduct. Initiatives to address these shortcomings, either through regulation, administrative reform, or government-sponsored voluntary codes of conduct, have made little headway in countering endemic corruption. More transparent implementation of customs, taxation, licensing and other administrative regulations is necessary.

National Treatment

The 1999 Investment Law codifies principles of national treatment for foreign investors, including the right to purchase securities, transfer property rights, pursue rights in Russian courts, repatriate funds abroad after payment of duties and taxes, and receive compensation for nationalizations or illegal acts of Russian government bodies. However, the law goes on to state that federal law may provide for a number of exceptions, including, where necessary, for "the protection of the constitution, public morals and health, and the rights and lawful interest of other persons and the defense of the state." Thus, a large number of broadly-defined exceptions give the Russian government considerable discretion in prohibiting or inhibiting foreign investment. The law provides a "grandfather clause" that stipulates that existing 'priority' foreign investment projects with foreign participation of over 25 percent be protected from unforeseeable changes in the tax regime or new limitations on foreign investment. The law defines "priority" projects as those with a foreign charter capital of more than $4.1 million and with a total investment of more than $41 million. However, the lack of corresponding tax and customs regulations means that any protection afforded investors by this clause is only theoretical.

Foreign investment in businesses engaged in production and distribution of distilled spirits is limited to 49 percent. Foreign investment in the electrical power giant, Unified Energy Systems (UES), is limited to 25 percent. In practice, these limits have been exceeded, and there is discussion of whether to eliminate or raise the limits. The sale of UES subsidiaries began with the first Wholesale Generating Company selling 14.4 percent of its shares in November 2006. UES officials say that foreign companies are welcome to participate in the tenders as more power generation assets are put on the market in 2007.

Drafts of a new Law on Strategic Sectors have shown that foreign investment in the following sectors may be subject to prohibition and/or more burdensome approval requirements: enterprises in the nuclear industry or involved in handling radioactive materials; enterprises involved in work on infectious diseases; arms, munitions and military equipment production, maintenance or repair; the aviation and space industries; data-transmission infrastructure; production and distribution of encryption technologies and equipment; and production and sales of goods and providing services under conditions of a "natural monopoly" (e.g., activities such as operating certain gas networks); among others sectors. This draft law may be submitted to the Duma in 2007.

Taxes

In response to investor concerns over the arbitrary and heavy-handed application of the tax code, the Russian government initiated a package of tax reforms in 2005 that was designed to limit aggressive tax collection practices while lowering the overall tax burden. The Duma continues to work on a series of measures that are expected to introduce tax benefits for the high technology sector, protect the rights of investors with licenses to work in the energy sector, and raise the transparency of the tax audit process. The corporate profit tax has been 24 percent since 2002.

Regions and municipalities have the authority to grant exemptions to the regional portion of profits taxes. Regions are not able to grant individual tax exemptions.

Companies report that VAT refunds to a Russia-based exporter, which should be provided within three months after a claim is submitted, often do not occur on time, with customs and tax authorities applying a number of burdensome additional requirements. In addition, input VAT is often not refunded for a number of reasons, forcing exporters to seek court enforcement VAT refunds on exports are also the source of significant fraud, making it that much more difficult for legitimate exporters to obtain refunds. Legislation to simplify VAT reimbursements took effect on January 1, 2007. Under the new law, VAT refund processing time is expected to fall from three months to two weeks. In addition, during the course of their audits, Federal Tax Service officials will have the authority to confiscate improperly disbursed VAT refunds, with penalties.

Duties on the production and export of oil, which are generally quite high, have been adjusted several times over the past few years. In 2003, new legislation restored full discretion to the Russian government in establishing export duties on refined petroleum products. Changes in the tax code in 2004 shifted the burden away from manufacturing and services and towards the energy sector. In 2006, the Russian government passed legislation that will put into place a differentiated tax regime on oil production for certain regions to help address the recent trend of slowing growth in oil production.

Energy Sector

In 2006, the Russian government decided to initiate amendments to the current Law on Subsoil Use rather than pursue the entirely new law it had been working on for several years. In these amendments, the Russian government may include language that would restrict foreign company participation to minority stakes in certain "strategic" fields, including the activity of natural resource extraction. The proposed amendments indicate that foreigners can only participate as a minority in a strategic field development.

The Russian government recently opened up its two key energy firms – Gazprom and Rosneft – to wider participation by non-state investors. In December 2005, the government eliminated the Gazprom "ringfence" – the cap on foreign share ownership in the company. Gazprom has been acquiring other assets in related industries (electrical generation and oil) and has teamed up with Russia's largest coal producer in what appears to be an effort to create a national champion in the energy sector. In addition, several major oil companies are working out the terms for joint exploration and development of large gas fields under Gazprom's control. In July 2006, the Russian government held an initial public offering on the London Exchange for the oil company, Rosneft.

The Russian government will not enter into any further Production Sharing Agreements (PSAs - designed for energy projects that require high capital expenditure and a long period before profits or significant tax revenues are generated). Prior to 2003, three PSA regimes were in place: the Sakhalin I and II consortia, and Kharyaga. This year, the operator of Sakhalin II, Sakhalin Energy, has been subject to criticism by the government for alleged environmental violations that occurred during pipeline construction. The members of the Sakhalin Energy consortium (led by Royal Dutch Shell) entered into discussions with the Russian government which resulted in the consortium agreeing to reduce its stake and giving Gazprom a controlling share.

In addition, the Caspian Pipeline Consortium (CPC) project, operational as of 2001, continues to seek authorization from the Russian government to allow expansion of the pipeline's capacity. (Pipeline expansion requires unanimous approval from the 11 shareholders in the consortium.) Final agreement could come in 2007.

Aviation

Many of the Russian-flagged carriers have aging fleets and use outmoded avionics and engines, but several are seriously considering significant purchases or wet-leases of foreign aircraft in an attempt to be more competitive with Western airlines. Russia's aircraft manufacturers only produce ten planes per year on average and therefore cannot keep up with Russian airlines' projected demand for 1500 additional planes in the next twenty years.

Current Russian law stipulates preferential treatment (tax holidays, guarantees on investment, etc.) for Russian and foreign investors in aviation-related research and manufacturing ventures. However, it limits the share of foreign capital in aviation enterprises to less than 25 percent and requires that board members and senior management staff be Russian citizens. There is speculation that the 25 percent limit could be raised or eliminated to make way for further investment.

The government is also looking to reorganize and revitalize Russia's aircraft industry in the context of a larger restructuring plan for Russia's defense industry. Civil aviation and the aircraft manufacturing industry are under considerable Russian government scrutiny following three major airplane crashes in 2006. Large-scale consolidation of the aircraft industry took place with the government creation of the Unified Aircraft Corporation (UAC). The Russian government expects the UAC to fulfill no fewer than twenty contracts in the next year for helicopters, sports planes and engines (worth approximately $380 million). The UAC is already negotiating with European Aeronautic Defence and Space Company (EADS) for long term design contract work and a possible joint-venture on the next generation of Airbus jets, and in 2006, the Russian government acquired 5 percent of EADS.

Capital Flows

On July 1, 2006, Russia began allowing the free flow of capital into and out of its financial system. The Central Bank no longer maintains either minimum-time requirements on capital flows or mandatory reserve requirements on the movement of capital.

ELECTRONIC COMMERCE

Electronic commerce exceeded forecasted growth in 2006, increasing from approximately $1 billion in 2005 to over $1.2 billion in the first six months of 2006. The volume is growing at a brisk pace and is expected to continue, though in comparison to many other countries, electronic commerce remains an embryonic market in Russia. The number of stores on the Russian Internet is estimated at only 2,000 to 4,000, and many do not accept on-line payments, merely using their websites for cash on delivery requests. Although Internet access in Russia is growing steadily, penetration is less than 20 percent of the population, with over 30 percent of these users located in the Moscow and St. Petersburg regions.

On January 1, 2005, the "Law on the Protection of Consumer Rights" took effect, which allows consumers a seven-day period to return goods purchased online. The "Law on Personal Data" came into effect in July 2006, and provides for the protection of consumer information. A draft law on electronic trade has been stalled in the Duma for several years. While closely following an International Chamber of Commerce model bill, it has significant problems, including the fact that it limits electronic transactions to the sale and purchase of moveable goods, services agreements, and shipments.

Russian law does not currently provide identical legislative protection for both electronic and paper documents. Because of this discrepancy, electronic settlement of outstanding charges is problematic, and currency control provisions may apply when paying in a currency other than rubles. The tax effect of electronic commerce is virtually unexplored, and this area of the law is still developing.

Registered trademarks are not recognized in Russia as entailing rights to the equivalent domain names. This has led to cases of cyber-squatting where intellectual property rights infringers register domain names that are identical or similar to established trademarks in hopes of illicit financial gain. The courts have taken divergent approaches to litigation arising from such disputes. The new Part IV of the Civil Code, which will replace the existing Russian intellectual property rights laws after January 1, 2008, contains provisions that address this issue, although it is difficult to tell at this juncture whether it may indeed correct the problem.

A law on electronic digital signatures went into effect on January 14, 2002. This law does not follow the Model Law on Electronic Signatures of the U.N. Commission on International Trade Law, but rather defines electronic signatures strictly, making public-key technology the sole acceptable digital signature technology. It also requires that hardware and software used in digital signature authentication programs be certified in Russia. This gives the Russian government the right to insist on the decompilation of electronic signature programs. These requirements, in addition to the aforementioned licensing requirements related to goods with encryption technology, present serious obstacles to trade in goods that Russia requires for further development of electronic commerce.

OTHER BARRIERS

The U.S. logging industry reports that illegal logging accounts for as much as 20 percent to 30 percent of Russia's timber harvest. Illegal wood supplies have begun to appear in China, hurting U.S. exports to that market. Illegal logging continues to increase, particularly in the Far East due to its proximity to China.

According to World Wildlife Fund data, the share of unregistered wood to total volume of timber consumption is 53 percent in Chita region, 34 percent in Primorskiy kray, 33 percent in Khabarovsk kray, 17 percent in Vologda region, and 10 percent in Krasnoyarsk kray.

In: Trade Barriers in Europe
Editor: Paula R. Lignelli, pp. 99-105

ISBN: 978-1-60021-956-6
© 2007 Nova Science Publishers, Inc.

Chapter 5

SWITZERLAND

TRADE SUMMARY

The U.S. goods trade balance with Switzerland went from a trade deficit of $2.3 billion in 2005 to a trade surplus of $137 million in 2006. U.S. goods exports in 2006 were $14.4 billion, up 34.1 percent from the previous year. Corresponding U.S. imports from Switzerland were $14.2 billion, up 9.5 percent. Switzerland is currently the 16th largest export market for U.S. goods.

U.S. exports of private commercial services (i.e., excluding military and government) to Switzerland were $9.5 billion in 2005 (latest data available), and U.S. imports were $11.4 billion. Sales of services in Switzerland by majority U.S.-owned affiliates were $9.1 billion in 2004 (latest data available), while sales of services in the United States by majority Switzerland-owned firms were $34.4 billion.

The stock of U.S. foreign direct investment (FDI) in Switzerland in 2005 was $83.4 billion, down from $106.8 billion in 2004. U.S. FDI in Switzerland is concentrated largely in the non-bank holding companies, manufacturing, wholesale trade and banking sectors.

IMPORT POLICIES

Agricultural Products

Although agriculture retains an important role in society and a strong lobby among politicians, the sector has been losing its relative importance in the Swiss economy for some time. Preservation of the Swiss agricultural sector is largely due to governmental intervention and support. While the average tariff for manufactured products is 2.3 percent, the simple average tariff in Switzerland on imports of agricultural products ranges from 28.6 percent to 36.2 percent. Switzerland is a relatively difficult market in which few U.S. agricultural products can successfully compete. This is due to high tariffs on certain agricultural products, preferential tariff rates for other countries, and government regulation and negative public perception of agricultural products derived from biotechnology. High tariffs and quotas are a direct cause of the modest levels of U.S. wheat, corn and soybean exports. The U.S. share of the Swiss agricultural import market in 2004 was 3 percent. Imports of nearly all agriculture products, no matter the country of origin, are subject to import duties and quotas.

Agricultural tariff-rate quotas present problems for U.S. exporters, as Swiss regulations often allocate quotas and incentives to importers that use their imports as inputs for domestic products. This practice has increased protection for domestic producers and in some cases, such as potato products, has effectively blocked U.S. exports. Swiss regulations and public resistance to agricultural products derived from biotechnology or the use of growth hormones remains strong, and, partially as a result, U.S. agricultural exports to Switzerland during 2004 dropped by 29 percent by volume and by 5.9 percent by value.

Hormone-treated beef became an issue in 2006 after the Swiss State Secretariat for Economic Affairs (SECO) and the Federal Veterinary (BVET) notified the World Trade Organization (WTO) in August that Switzerland would begin requiring European Union (EU) animal health certificates for imported livestock products effective April 1, 2007. This action is tied to Switzerland's planned harmonization of animal health rules with the EU and the future end of veterinary border controls between Switzerland and the EU. However, since hormone-treated beef is not allowed in the EU, the proposed Swiss rules would effectively end U.S. beef exports to Switzerland, estimated to have been approximately 300 tons in 2005. Switzerland has postponed implementation of this measure for the time being. The U.S. and Swiss governments are discussing the proposed Swiss harmonization with EU animal health regulations in an effort to find a solution that will allow trade in U.S. beef to continue.

As of January 2000, imports of fresh meat and eggs produced in a manner not permitted for products produced in Switzerland must be clearly labeled as such. Methods not allowed in Switzerland include the use of growth hormones, antibiotics and other substances in the raising of beef and pork, as well as the production of eggs from chickens kept in certain types of cages.

The Swiss Veterinary Agency continues to refuse to list new U.S. facilities as eligible to export beef to Switzerland and, despite repeated requests, has not produced science-based reasons for this position. Swiss inaction has blocked three facilities that the United States requested be listed since early 2002. The Swiss government has made clear that the situation is related to its dissatisfaction with current U.S. regulations that block certain Swiss processed beef exports to the United States due to concerns over Bovine Spongiform Encephalopathy (BSE) and foot-and-mouth disease.

Biotechnology

Switzerland has taken a case-by-case approach to agricultural products derived from biotechnology since voters rejected a moratorium on biotechnology research and products in 1998. Agricultural biotechnology products must be certified by the Federal Office of Public Health, and the manufacturer of such products must submit detailed information concerning the product development process. Swiss authorities review each product for toxicity, resistance to antibiotics and allergenic characteristics. However, industry has noted that the approval process is lengthy and burdensome in comparison with other countries' approval systems. Once a product is approved, its certificate for approval is valid for five years, after which a product must repeat the approval process.

Switzerland has required labeling for foods containing products derived from biotechnology since 1996. In January 2005, the federal government lowered the labeling threshold for agricultural products derived from biotechnology from 1.0 percent to 0.9 percent in order to harmonize its regulations with those of the EU. A notable exception to the labeling requirement is the use of substances such as soy oil in the production process. According to Swiss officials, these ingredients do not require a label because testing cannot show they are derived from bio-engineered commodities.

The animal feed industry has succeeded in establishing a small market in Switzerland for products derived from biotechnology. However, the planting of seed crops derived from biotechnology faces difficult environmental approval hurdles. Despite opposition by the Swiss government, voters adopted a popular initiative "Food from GMO-free Agriculture" in November 2005 that introduced a five year moratorium on commercial planting of crops derived from biotechnology. Swiss authorities have noted that requests for the commercial planting of such crops after the moratorium is over can be submitted and would be considered during the moratorium period. The initiative should have little impact on trade in agricultural products derived from biotechnology because the moratorium applies to domestic plantings; whereas existing Swiss legislation still permits their importation.

The government has stated that the five-year moratorium did not require implementing legislation and took effect immediately. The moratorium does not contain provisions on scientific research in this area; the government pledged SFr12 million ($9.1 million) for a national research program to study the uses and possible risks of agricultural products derived from biotechnology.

GOVERNMENT PROCUREMENT

Switzerland is a signatory of the WTO Government Procurement Agreement (GPA). On the cantonal and local levels, a law passed by Parliament in 1995 provides for non-discriminatory access to government procurement.

In 2004, the Swiss government initiated a series of informal consultations to amend the Swiss Federal Law on Public Procurement. Ultimately, this process should simplify the public tender procedure and harmonize the many different cantonal tender procedures. Under the GPA, Swiss cantons are allowed to implement the GPA independently from the federal government, which sometimes leads to different procedures among cantons.

In general, quality and technical criteria are as important as price in the evaluation of tenders. Cantons and communes usually prefer local suppliers because they can recover part of their outlays through income taxes paid by the suppliers. Foreign firms may be required to guarantee technical support and after-sale service if they have no local office or representation.

Notices of Swiss government tenders at the federal level are published in the Swiss Official Gazette of Commerce and on the on-line Swiss government procurement website. There is no requirement that bids be submitted by a local agent.

INTELLECTUAL PROPERTY RIGHTS (IPR) PROTECTION

In general, Switzerland maintains exceptionally high standards of protection of intellectual property rights. Certain concerns have been expressed, however, with respect to the development of revised copyright legislation that would, among other purposes, conclude Switzerland's accession to the WIPO Copyright Treaty and the WIPO Performances and Phonograms Treaty. These concerns have focused on the potential for this revised legislation to allow an overly broad ability to circumvent technological protection measures intended to protect copyrighted material. The United States will continue to monitor this legislation.

SERVICES BARRIERS

Telecommunications

The 1998 Telecommunications Act brought liberalization and privatization to the Swiss telecommunications sector, opening the market to investment and competition from foreign firms. More than 50 Swiss and foreign companies now offer fixed line services. Three different operators, Swisscom, Sunrise (TeleDanmark), and Orange (France Telecom) provide mobile telephone services, and each company also owns third-generation mobile telephony licenses. Until 2005, SBC Communications' 9.5 percent stake in Sunrise's parent company represented the only significant U.S. presence in the Swiss telecommunications market.

In October 2005, U.S. Liberty Global purchased 100 percent of the shares of Cablecom, the largest cable (phone and Internet) operator in Switzerland and second-largest Internet service provider behind Swisscom – the incumbent state monopoly. Stiff competition between the two operators has already led to a sharp drop in fixed line rates.

Swisscom continues to use litigation to block the Swiss government's efforts to open the telecommunications market to competition. For example, Swisscom has successfully fought efforts by the Competition Commission and the Federal Communications Commission (ComCom) to unbundle the local loop and provide leased lines at cost-oriented prices. In response, the government is in the process of creating additional legal authority for the regulator to implement these initiatives. In October 2004, the lower house of the Parliament began work on amending the Telecom Act to give the regulator explicit authority to force Swisscom to unbundle its local loop, effectively fixing the "flaw" cited by the federal court. The reform will cover only fixed line services and will not extend to other technologies, such as mobile and WiFi. The bill also requires that broadband access be offered to Swisscom competitors at cost-oriented prices over a period of six years, after which all operators are expected to have broadband investments themselves. In 2005, Swisscom lowered its interconnection prices by 7 percent and announced a further 5 percent drop for 2006.

In October 2004, ComCom opened an investigation into Swisscom's broadband access pricing on the grounds that it might give preferential rates to its Internet subsidiary "Bluewin" in comparison with its competitors. This is not the first time the competition watchdog has investigated Swisscom's broadband practices. In 2003, it ordered Swisscom to stop giving preferential discounts to Bluewin. Because of Swisscom's monopoly on the last mile, fixed-line competitors have no choice but to deal with the company if they desire to enter the Swiss market.

Audiovisual Services

Switzerland has no limitations on the amount of non-Swiss or non-European origin programming that can be broadcast, but film distributors and cinema companies must maintain, through self-regulatory solutions, an "appropriate diversity" – not currently defined – in the products offered within a region. The government may levy a nominal development tax on movie theater tickets if the Swiss government determines the appropriate diversity is not being met. The development tax receipts will be used to finance new theaters that could offer greater diversity in the films being shown within a region. Switzerland is a signatory of the October 2005 UNESCO Convention on Cultural Diversity.

Postal Services

The Postal Act divides the Swiss postal market into two segments – universal services and competitive services. Competitive services, which include express delivery, are unrestricted. Universal services are divided into reserved and non-reserved services. Only Swiss Post is required to provide universal service. Swiss Post is the exclusive provider of reserved services, while it competes with private postal operators for the provision of non-reserved services. Private postal operators are allowed to provide specific non-reserved services (shipment and handling of out-bound international mail, and of addressed packages of up to 20 kg) subject to a license, provided they can ensure regular and professional shipment of mail and parcels and reach a turnover, subject to value-added tax, of at least SFr100,000. PostReg, the regulatory authority, exercises market supervision, ensures the functioning and fair competition in the postal market, and enables the proper implementation of applicable regulations. Postal restrictions on parcel deliveries were lifted in 2004, and letters sent abroad or for which the delivery costs were more than SFr5 ($4) could also be sent by other companies.

In April 2006, the Swiss government reduced Swiss Post's monopoly from the current 350-gram threshold to 100 grams. The government's decision to liberalize the market further was based on an independent study which confirmed that a further liberalization of letter delivery services would not disrupt the country's mail distribution, a key issue for voters. Efforts by the Swiss business community to lower Swiss Post's monopoly to 50 grams or grant unlimited access to competitors failed to reach a consensus in the Swiss parliament. The government is expected to publish a report in 2007 on ways to liberalize further the letter delivery service. Swiss trade unions have warned that any further opening of the market should not go beyond what was approved by parliament three years ago.

Insurance

With the highest per capita insurance expenditure in the world, Switzerland's insurance market is extremely appealing to foreign competitors. Of the 198 insurance companies currently operating in the Swiss market, at least 40 are foreign subsidiaries. Of the 198 companies, 26 offer life insurance, 117 offer non-life insurance and approximately 55 offer reinsurance. Foreign companies offering only reinsurance are not subject to oversight by the supervisory body, the Federal Office of Private Insurance (FOPI).

However, barriers to foreign insurance entry still persist. Foreign insurers attempting to do business in Switzerland are required to establish a subsidiary or a branch and cannot sell their entire product line cross-border or through a representative office. Foreign insurers operating in Switzerland are limited to those types of insurance for which they are licensed in their home countries. The manager of the foreign-owned branch must be resident in Switzerland and the majority of the board of directors of the Swiss subsidiary must have citizenship in the European Free Trade Association (Switzerland, Norway, Iceland and Liechtenstein). Public monopolies exist for fire and natural damage insurance in 19 cantons, and for the insurance of workplace accidents in certain industries. Private insurance firms must establish a fund – amounting to between 20 percent and 50 percent of their minimum capital requirement – available at short notice to cover potential losses. A new insurance law took effect on January 1, 2006, that increases the solvency requirements of all insurance companies operating in Switzerland. As part of a bilateral agreement with the European Union, EU non-life insurers are not required to deposit a certain percentage of their assets with the Swiss National Bank (SNB). However, non-EU life-insurers are required to do so.

INVESTMENT BARRIERS

Switzerland welcomes foreign investment and accords national treatment to all foreign investors. The federal government's approach is to create and maintain general conditions that are favorable both to Swiss and foreign investors. Swiss banking laws encourage the formation of abundant pools of capital from overseas investors. Some cantons have income tax incentive programs to encourage foreign investment.

There is no screening of foreign investment, except for investments in land ownership and national security investments, nor are there any sectoral or geographical preferences or restrictions. Cantons have been granted extensive decision-making powers with respect to foreigners' purchases of land. Investment restrictions related to national security apply to hydroelectric and nuclear power, operation of oil pipelines, transportation of explosive materials, operation of airlines and marine navigation.

ANTICOMPETITIVE PRACTICES

The Swiss economy has long been characterized by a high degree of cartelization, primarily among domestically-oriented firms and industries. In June 2003, the Swiss parliament adopted a revised competition bill, which took effect on April 1, 2004. The most significant improvement is authority to prosecute anticompetitive behavior without prior warning, with a maximum fine of 10 percent of a firm's total combined revenue for the past three years. Companies that cooperate with regulators are eligible for a reduced fine.

Electricity

Electricity production is competitive, but local public monopolies dominate electricity transmission and distribution within Switzerland. Several cantons have attempted to prevent other providers from serving their areas, but those efforts were ruled illegal under the Cartel Law. Local communities as a result have tried to bypass the federal court ruling by cementing their dominant position through cantonal legislative changes or "gentlemen's agreements" with large customers.

During a referendum initiated by Swiss labor unions in 2002, the population rejected a bill aimed at permitting third party access throughout the grid. But experts argue that lower energy power prices in neighboring countries will at some point force Switzerland to adapt. The Swiss government has recently proposed another electricity bill to liberalize the market. The first phase – scheduled to start in 2007 – will allow commercial users to choose their electricity supplier. The bill provides for the unbundling of transmission from commercial activities, the merger of transmission operators into a single system knows as "Swissgrid," and establishes an independent regulatory agency for the electricity sector. A second phase will provide for full market liberalization in 2012.

Chapter 6

TURKEY

TRADE SUMMARY

The U.S. goods trade balance with Turkey went from a trade deficit of $913 million in 2005 to a trade surplus of $366 million in 2006. U.S. goods exports in 2006 were $5.7 billion, up 34.2 percent from the previous year. Corresponding U.S. imports from Turkey were $5.4 billion, up 3.5 percent. Turkey is currently the 30th largest export market for U.S. goods.

The stock of U.S. foreign direct investment (FDI) in Turkey in 2005 was $2.4 billion (latest data available), the same as in 2004. U.S. FDI in Turkey is concentrated largely in the banking, wholesale and manufacturing sectors.

IMPORT POLICIES

Tariffs and Quantitative Restrictions

Turkey applies the EU's common external customs tariff to third-country (including the United States) non-agricultural imports and imposes no duty on non-agricultural items from EU and European Free Trade Association (EFTA) countries.

Turkey maintains high tariff rates (25 percent average most-favored-nation rate) on many food and agricultural product imports. The Turkish government often increases tariffs on grains during the domestic harvest. High feed prices harm Turkish livestock industries, particularly for beef and poultry. Duties on fresh fruits range from 15.4 percent to 145.8 percent. Tariffs on processed fruit, fruit juice, and vegetables range between 19.5 percent and 130 percent. The Turkish government also levies high duties, excise taxes and other domestic charges on imported alcoholic beverages that increase wholesale prices by more than 200 percent.

Import Licenses and other Restrictions

Import licenses are required for products that need after-sales service (e.g., photocopiers, advanced data processing equipment and diesel generators), distilled spirits and agricultural products. Lack of transparency in Turkey's import licensing system can result in costly delays, demurrage charges and other uncertainties that stifle trade for many agricultural products and for distilled spirits. In November 2005, the United States brought a dispute against Turkey in the World Trade Organization (WTO) arguing that, *inter alia*, Turkey's tariff-rate quota (TRQ) scheme, which contains an onerous domestic purchase requirement, and its refusal to issue import licenses outside the TRQ, are inconsistent with Turkey's WTO obligations. This case is proceeding through WTO dispute settlement.

In some cases, notably for meat and poultry (not to mention over-quota imports of rice), the Turkish government simply does not issue licenses, thereby creating a *de facto* ban on imports of these products. Turkey has not allowed livestock for slaughter or meat imports from any foreign country since 1996 and has not established any public health requirements for the entry of meat. Outbreaks of Bovine Spongiform Encephalopathy (BSE) and foot and mouth disease (FMD) in Europe strengthened Turkey's resolve to keep livestock and meat products out of its market. The United States is currently not able to export breeding livestock to Turkey since the EU placed the United States in the third BSE risk category. Turkey's BSE Committee has decided not to import any breeding cattle from category 3 countries (based on the EU system). The United States is also unable to export poultry meat for consumption within Turkey because the government of Turkey requires its officials to inspect and approve all foreign processing facilities and expects inspection costs to be covered by Turkish importers.

Due to the EU accession process, Turkey is in the process of rewriting its agriculture import regulations in order to harmonize them with the EU. Some new regulations, especially sanitary and phytosanitary measures and reference price systems, do not appear to be applied in an EU-consistent manner.

Despite liberalization of the spirits and tobacco markets, including a completed privatization of the state-owned alcoholic beverage company and plans to privatize the state-owned tobacco company, as well as privatization of imports of wine and alcoholic beverages, increases in consumption have been inhibited by inordinately high tariffs (85 percent - 100 percent) and special consumption taxes (275 percent), along with the value-added-tax (VAT). In 2006, legislation was introduced to reduce the number of control certificates required to import distilled spirits from two to one.

STANDARDS, TESTING, LABELING AND CERTIFICATION

The Turkish government has a poor track record of notifying WTO Members of proposed technical regulations and phytosanitary requirements, and implementation can appear to be arbitrary. Importers report increasing difficulty in obtaining information on sanitary and phytosanitary certifications. The Turkish government often requires laboratory testing on items not normally subject to testing by trading partners. U.S. imports could increase by an estimated $10 million to $25 million if these procedures were regularized.

U.S. companies have reported that products with the EU certificate of conformity (CE mark), particularly medical devices, have been detained by Turkish customs authorities for inspection. In some cases, U.S. products apparently have been subjected to additional tests, despite their CE marks. The Turkish government believes that it has addressed these complaints. For importation of distilled spirits, Customs requires that between 2 and 4 bottles per consignment be submitted for unspecified analysis, raising the cost of importing.

GOVERNMENT PROCUREMENT

Turkey is not a signatory to the WTO Agreement on Government Procurement; however, it is an observer to the WTO Committee on Government Procurement. Although Turkey's laws require competitive bidding procedures for tenders, U.S. companies have complained that they can be lengthy and overly complicated.

Turkey's public tender law established an independent board to oversee public tenders. Foreign companies can participate in state tenders that are above an established threshold. The law provides a price preference of up to 15 percent for domestic bidders, which is not available if they form a joint venture with foreign bidders. Turkey has expanded the definition of domestic bidder to include foreign-owned corporate entities established under Turkish law.

Military procurement generally includes an offset requirement in the tender specifications. The offset guidelines were recently modified to encourage foreign direct investment and technology transfer.

EXPORT SUBSIDIES

Turkey employs a number of incentives to promote exports, although programs have been scaled back in recent years to comply with EU directives and WTO commitments. Historically, wheat and sugar have been Turkey's main subsidized commodities. Export subsidies, ranging from 10 percent to 20 percent of export values, are granted to 16 agricultural or processed agricultural products. In 2004, the Turkish Grain Board (TMO) sold domestic wheat at world prices (well below domestic prices) to Turkish flour and pasta manufacturers based upon their exports of flour and pasta. The Turkish Export-Import Bank provides exporters with credits, guarantees and insurance programs. Certain tax credits also are available to exporters.

INTELLECTUAL PROPERTY RIGHTS (IPR) PROTECTION

Turkey's intellectual property rights regime has improved in recent years, but still contains serious problems. Turkey remained on the Special 301 "Priority Watch List" in 2006 due to concerns about the lack of protection for confidential test data submitted by pharmaceutical companies against unfair commercial use and continued high levels of piracy and counterfeiting of copyright and trademark materials. Turkey is a signatory to a number of international conventions, including the Stockholm Act of the Paris Convention, the Patent Cooperation Treaty and the Strasbourg Agreement.

Turkey's copyright law provides deterrent penalties for infringement. It does not, however, prohibit circumvention of technical protection measures, a key feature of the World Intellectual Property Organization (WIPO) "Internet" treaties. Generally, Turkish courts have not imposed deterrent penalties on pirates as provided in the copyright law but have instead applied the Turkish Cinema Law, which has much lower penalties. More recently, Turkish courts have issued increasingly severe sentences for copyright infringers, but significant backlogs in the courts slow redress. Recently enacted legislation contains several strong anti-piracy provisions, including a ban on street sales of all copyright products and authorization for law enforcement authorities to take action without a complaint by the rights holder. But the law also reduces potential prison sentences for piracy convictions.

In accordance with the 1995 patent law and a Turkish agreement with the EU, patent protection for pharmaceuticals began on January 1, 1999. Turkey has been accepting patent applications since 1996 in compliance with the TRIPS agreement "mailbox" provisions. The patent law does not, however, contain interim protection for pharmaceuticals in the research and development "pipeline."

Turkey's recently amended Patent Law provides for penalties for infringement of up to three years in prison, or approximately $32,000 in fines, or both, and closure of the business for up to one year. Research-based companies in the pharmaceuticals sector are concerned about provisions that delay the initiation of infringement suits until after the patent is approved and published, permit use of a patented invention to generate data needed for the marketing approval of generic pharmaceutical products and give judges wider discretion over penalties in infringement cases. Turkey does not currently have a system for patent linkage; the lack of such a system could create confusion and possibly allow generic pharmaceutical manufacturers to obtain marketing approval for a patent-infringing copy of a brand name drug.

The Ministry of Health introduced limited protection for undisclosed test data against unfair commercial use in a regulation issued in January 2005 and revised in June 2005. However, several of the regulation's provisions severely undermine protection for confidential test data. Data protection is limited to original products licensed in a European Union member country after January 1, 2001, for which no generic manufacturers had applied for licenses in Turkey as of January 1, 2005. The term of exclusivity is limited to the duration of the drug patent or to six years after the date of licensing in a European Customs Union country, implying a shorter term of protection because of the length of the marketing approval process in Turkey. Research-based companies estimate that, due to the prolonged regulatory review, on average the period of data protection is diminished by 20 percent to 25 percent.

Trademark holders also contend that there is widespread and often sophisticated counterfeiting of their marks in Turkey, especially in apparel, film, cosmetics, detergent and other products.

SERVICES BARRIERS

Telecommunications Services

In 2005, Turkey committed to end Turk Telecom's exclusive rights on phone telephony and other basic telecommunications services by 2006. It also made a commitment to provide immediate market access for data transmission services. In line with earlier commitments to WTO, Turkey opened its cellular mobile services and paging to competition.

In November 2005, 55 percent of the government-owned Turk Telecom was sold to a foreign investor. Turk Telecom still dominates the markets for value-added services, including Internet services. The Telecommunications Authority (TK), which reports to the Ministry of Transport, is slowly gaining experience and greater authority. Applicable licensing regulations are published on the Authority's website.

Other Services Barriers

There are restrictions on establishment in financial services, the petroleum sector, broadcasting and maritime transportation (see Investment Barriers section). Turkey restricts the ability of doctors, attorneys and other professionals to practice their professions. Legislation awaiting final approval by Parliament would permit foreign doctors to work in Turkey.

INVESTMENT BARRIERS

The United States-Turkey Bilateral Investment Treaty (BIT) entered into force in May 1990. Turkey has a liberal investment regime, but private investment has historically been hindered by excessive bureaucracy, political and macroeconomic uncertainty, a weak judicial system, high tax rates, a weak framework for corporate governance, and frequent changes in the legal and regulatory environment. Turkey has enjoyed several successive years of economic growth and stability which has contributed to a substantial increase in foreign direct investment. The corporate tax rate was reduced from 30 percent to 20 percent and new regulations were enacted that make it possible to establish a business in Turkey in one day. Turkish government policy is to encourage foreign direct investment.

Almost all areas open to investment by the Turkish private sector are fully open to foreign participation without screening or prior approval, although establishment in the financial and petroleum sectors requires special permission. Foreign equity ownership is limited to 25 percent in broadcasting and 49 percent in maritime transportation. Parliament is considering draft legislation easing restrictions on foreign ownership in the media sector. Once investors have committed to the Turkish market, they have sometimes found their investments undermined by legislative action, such as the imposition of production limits. One example of such limitations is the sugar law, which sets the price for domestically-produced sugar well above the world market price, limits the domestic production of fructose and, thus, creates a shortage of domestically-produced fructose. The law also sets a duty on imported fructose of 135 percent.

The Turkish government accepts binding international arbitration of investment disputes between foreign investors and the state. A recent law expanded the scope of international arbitration in contracts with the Turkish government. Investors continue to have concerns about the government's recognition and enforcement of arbitral awards against public entities, and at least one American company reports that the judicial system in Turkey has not recognized foreign arbitral awards. Turkey is a party to both the United Nations Convention on the Recognition and Enforcement of Foreign Arbitral Awards and the ICSID Convention.

Turkish law calls for a liberalized energy market in which private firms are able to develop projects with the approval of the Energy Market Regulatory Authority, an independent regulatory body. The state electricity utility has been unbundled into production, transmission, distribution and trading companies, but little progress has been made in privatizing power generation and distribution. The Privatization Agency announced a tender for three electricity distribution regions in late August 2006, however the privatization was postponed in January 2007 until after the November parliamentary elections. Liberalization in the natural gas sector has also faced delays. The state pipeline company, BOTAS, will remain dominant, but legislation requires a phased transfer of 80 percent of its gas purchase contracts.

As the result of a 1997 court decision, the Turkish government has blocked full repatriation of profits by oil companies under Article 116 of the 1954 Petroleum Law, which protected foreign investors from the impact of lira depreciation. Affected companies have challenged the 1997 decision. The judgments in almost all such lawsuits have been against the claimant companies. A new petroleum law that seeks to provide greater investment incentives and protections still awaits passage in the parliament.

OTHER BARRIERS

Corruption

Turkey has ratified the OECD antibribery convention and passed implementing legislation providing that makes bribes of foreign officials, as well as domestic officials illegal and not tax deductible. Corruption is perceived to be a major problem in Turkey by private enterprises and the public at large, particularly by government officials and politicians. The judicial system is also perceived to be susceptible to external influence and to be biased against outsiders to some degree.

Energy

In 2001, the Turkish government cancelled 46 contracted power projects based on the Build-Operate-Transfer (BOT) and transfer-of-operating-rights models. Turkey's constitutional court ruled in 2002 that the government would have to either honor the contracts or compensate the companies involved. One of those companies has launched an international arbitration case. In 2002, the government requested BOT projects already in operation, which include U.S.-owned companies and/or creditors, to apply for new licenses from the new Energy Market Regulatory Authority (EMRA). Negotiations between the Turkish government and the relevant companies concerning the request of the Turkish government to reduce the electricity sale tariffs are continuing while the license application process is still underway. Despite lack of action on new licenses, the Turkish government has continued to purchase electricity produced under the existing contracts.

Taxes

Taxation of all cola drinks (raised in 2002 to 47.5 percent under Turkey's "Special Consumption Tax") discourages investment by major U.S. cola producers. Turkey assesses a special consumption tax of 27 percent to 50 percent on all motor vehicles based on engine size, which has a disproportionate effect on U.S. automobiles.

Corporate Governance

A recent OECD report stated that Turkey's overall corporate governance outlook is positive because the authorities have already adopted, or are introducing, high quality corporate governance standards (including audit standards) and because transparency has improved significantly. The report cautions, however, that it is important for Turkey to improve further in the areas of control and disclosure of related party transactions and self-dealing, the protection of minority shareholders, and the role of the board in overseeing not only management but also controlling shareholders.

Pharmaceuticals

Besides their intellectual property concerns detailed above, the pharmaceutical industry's sales have been affected by government price controls. Research-based industry is also concerned about achieving transparent and equitable treatment in upcoming reforms of the government's health care and pension system.

UKRAINE

TRADE SUMMARY

The U.S. goods trade deficit with Ukraine was $883 million in 2006, an increase of $318 million from $565 million in 2005. U.S. goods exports in 2006 were $756 million, up 41.9 percent from the previous year. Corresponding U.S. imports from Ukraine were $1.6 billion, up 49.3 percent. Ukraine is currently the 72nd largest export market for U.S. goods.

The stock of U.S. foreign direct investment (FDI) in Ukraine in 2005 was $356 million (latest data available), up from $256 million in 2004.

WTO ACCESSION

Ukraine is in the process of negotiating terms of accession to the World Trade Organization (WTO). On March 6, 2006, the United States and Ukraine signed a WTO bilateral market access agreement. Later that month, the United States terminated the application of the Jackson-Vanik amendment to the Trade Act of 1974 to Ukraine, providing Ukraine permanent normal trade relations (PNTR) status. The Ukrainian government has completed its bilateral market access negotiations with most other interested WTO Members, and is now focused on completing its implementation of WTO provisions and resolving remaining outstanding issues involving WTO rules. Ukraine must also complete negotiations on the levels of funding for certain programs supporting its agriculture sector. Ukraine made significant progress during 2006 in passing legislation needed for compliance with WTO requirements, enacting some 20 WTO-related laws in the fall of 2006 and adding to its steady progress in this area in the previous two years. Members of Ukraine's WTO accession Working Party, including the United States, are planning onward steps in the multilateral Working Party process for Ukraine's WTO accession.

IMPORT POLICIES

Ukraine continues to maintain fees and licensing requirements on certain imports. Ukraine imposes several duties and taxes on imported goods: customs/import tariffs, value-added-tax (VAT) and excise duties. Additionally, imports into Ukraine are subject to customs processing fees, a unified fee on vehicles crossing Ukraine's borders and port fees.

Customs/Import Tariffs

Ukraine's tariff schedule provides for two rates of import duty: full rates and Most Favored Nation (MFN) rates. The full rate of import duty can be from two to ten times higher than the MFN rate; it is applied to goods from 81 countries. Imports from the United States are subject to the MFN rate. Upon accession, Ukraine would apply the MFN rate to all goods originating from WTO Members, in accordance with Article I of the GATT 1994.

Import duties are calculated in accordance with the law "On the Customs Tariff of Ukraine" introduced in 2001, although their levels currently undergo frequent changes as a result of Ukraine's ongoing negotiations on WTO accession. The current customs tariff schedule comprises approximately 11,000 tariff lines. Most customs tariffs are levied at *ad valorem* rates, but 1,655 tariff line items (about 15 percent) are subject to specific and combined rates of duty. These specific and combined rates apply to approximately one-third of tariff-lines for agricultural goods, primarily those that are produced in Ukraine. These protected goods include grains, poultry products, sugar, and vegetables such as carrots and potatoes. In 2005, the Ukrainian Parliament, the Rada, passed amendments to the Customs Code of Ukraine, which decreased tariff rates in an effort to meet WTO accession requirements. The average applied tariff rate for all goods is now 6.5 percent. For agricultural goods, the average applied rate is 13.8 percent (down from 19.7 percent) and for industrial goods the average applied rate is 4.4 percent (down from 8.3 percent). Import tariffs were particularly high with respect to petroleum products; they were reduced, however, to zero during a summer 2005 shortage of gasoline and diesel fuel and have not increased again despite a number of proposals in the Rada.

High import tariffs on goods such as poultry act as a barrier to U.S. exports. As a result of the March 2006 WTO bilateral market access agreement with the United States, tariffs on poultry and many other goods will be reduced significantly when Ukraine joins the WTO.

In terms of customs-related issues affecting trade, imports of U.S. salmon roe (red caviar HS Code 0303 or 0305) were delayed when, early in 2005, the Ukrainian State Customs Service reclassified the products as fish roe substitute (HS Code 1604), which would require payment of a higher customs tariff. The State Customs Service requires court decisions to clear the products under the correct category, causing delays and leading to diminished U.S. exports of this highly perishable product.

Excise Duties

Ukraine applies excise duties to a limited set of goods imported into Ukraine, such as alcoholic beverages, non-filter cigarettes, motor vehicles and petroleum products. Most of the excise duties that established lower rates for domestically-produced goods than for imported goods were eliminated in 2005, but discriminatory excise duties still hinder U.S. exports of wine and grape spirits and automobiles to Ukraine. The excise duty rate on imported wine and grape spirits is 12 and 13 times higher, respectively, than on domestically-produced products, and is likely to remain at that level until Ukraine accedes to the WTO and excise rates on imported and domestic goods are unified. VAT and excise tax exemptions for locally-produced vehicles were eliminated on March 29, 2005. Excise taxes on automobiles remain high, ranging from 0.2 euros/cc for automobiles with smaller engines to 3 euros/cc for those with larger engines. Since the excise tax rate is based on the cubic capacity of the engine, it is biased against automobiles with larger engines. The import tariff on fully assembled automobiles was raised from 15 percent to 25 percent during 2005 to compensate local producers for the loss of VAT and excise privileges. This increase has negatively impacted importers of fully assembled automobiles, who are also disadvantaged since the tariff on semi-knocked down vehicles is lower.

Import Licenses

Import licenses are required for some goods, including pesticides, alcohol products, optical media production inputs, some industrial chemical products and equipment containing them, official foreign postage stamps, excise marks, officially stamped/headed paper, checks and securities, some goods that contain sensitive encryption technologies, and ozone-depleting substances. An importer is required to receive prior approval from the relevant administrative agency before receiving the necessary import license from the Ministry of Economy. Pursuant to the March 2006 U.S. bilateral market access agreement, Ukraine will not impose import licenses on imports of mass-market, commercially-traded goods containing encryption that are covered by the Information Technology Agreement. Additionally, in 2006, the Rada added fresh, chilled, or frozen beef and pork and related live animals to the list of goods subject to a form of automatic import licensing, where the requirement for prior approval from an administrative agency is waived. Poultry imports are already subject to such licensing.

For some goods, product certification is a prerequisite for an import license. Importers can certify the compliance of a foreign facility to Ukraine's technical regulations applied to imports. The U.S. distilled spirits industry reports that this option usually involves a burdensome visit and costly inspection by Ukrainian government officials. If approved, the supplier receives a certificate of conformity valid for two to three years, which avoids the burden of certification of each shipment, subjecting goods to mandatory laboratory tests upon arrival in Ukraine.

STANDARDS, TESTING, LABELING AND CERTIFICATION

For a number of years, U.S. investors regarded Ukraine's product certification system as a significant obstacle to trade and investment. U.S. businesses have complained that standards and certification requirements adversely affect their consumer goods exports. In January 2006, however, Ukraine's Parliament passed two new laws aimed at bringing Ukrainian practices in this area into line with the WTO Agreement on Technical Barriers to Trade. As of April 2006, more than 3,100 Ukrainian standards were harmonized with international standards, and approximately 8,000 remained to be harmonized.

Standardization and Certification

Mandatory certification is required in Ukraine for many products. The State Committee for Technical Regulation and Consumer Policy (DerzhSpozhyvStandard) is the standardization and certification body in Ukraine. DerzhSpozhyvStandard has a network of 115 accredited product certifying bodies including 53 accredited certifying bodies for quality management systems, as well as about 780 testing laboratories throughout Ukraine. Appropriate resources, such as modern analytical equipment and reactants, are not available in most laboratories. DerzhSpozhynStandard's system includes 27 territorial departments for consumer protection and 28 state centers for standardization, systematizing weights and measures, and certification. Depending on the type of product, testing and applicable certification scheme, the certification process can take from three days to one month.

Numerous certification bodies in Ukraine effectively operate as independent, often monopolistic, entities on a profit-making basis, returning just 20 percent of their fees to the state. Consequently, certification agencies do much of their regulatory work with little or no coordination with other Ukrainian bodies performing similar tests. Many products require multiple certificates from different agencies, with local, regional and municipal authorities often requesting additional documentation beyond that required by central bodies. According to industry sources, access to the Ukrainian market is impeded by numerous burdensome certification and licensing procedures for equipment. These issues are being addressed during Ukraine's WTO accession negotiations, and in recent years, Ukraine has reduced the number of products subject to mandatory certification. When Ukraine completes its implementation of the WTO Agreement on Technical Barriers to Trade when it accedes to the WTO, it will be obliged to apply such mandatory requirements only in conformity with WTO provisions on technical regulations (i.e., only in defense of human, animal and plant health and safety), and only based on sound science.

Sanitary and Phytosanitary (SPS) Measures

Ukraine has, in the past, applied a range of SPS measures that restrict imports of a number of U.S. agricultural products, among them, pork, beef and poultry. Ukraine's certification and approval process is lengthy, duplicative and expensive. In 2005, amendments to several laws, including the law "On Veterinary Medicine," and law "Quality and Safety of

Food Products and Food Raw Materials," were made to bring Ukrainian legislation into compliance with requirements of the WTO Agreement on the Application of Sanitary and Phytosanitary Measures. Further, legislation to bring Ukrainian law into compliance with international norms regarding veterinary medicine, standards, conformity assessment procedures and other sanitary and phytosanitary measures remain at various stages of drafting and consideration by Ukraine's Parliament. The following issues are subjects of discussion between the United States and Ukraine as part of Ukraine's accession to the WTO:

Beef, Beef Products and Pork

The March 2006 WTO bilateral market access agreement with the United States addresses the terms of U.S. exports of beef, beef products and pork to Ukraine. The two sides signed detailed veterinary certificates related to such goods. As agreed, Ukraine will allow the entry of certified U.S. beef and pork that meets veterinary certificate requirements. The United States is currently monitoring whether trade will be allowed to clear customs, as this is required for Ukraine to adhere to the bilateral commitments mentioned above.

In the past, Ukraine blocked the importation of beef and beef products due to concerns over the use of growth promoting hormones as well as bovine spongiform encephalopathy (BSE). The United States is working with Ukraine to ensure that any measures undertaken by Ukraine are consistent with World Organization for Animal Health (OIE) guidelines. Ukraine's Law of Veterinary Medicine is expected to address this issue.

U.S pork exports to Ukraine have been hampered by regulations concerning trichinae. The United States is working with Ukraine so that it takes the necessary steps to align Ukrainian standards for trichinae with international norms.

Biotechnology

Ukraine's biotechnology approval process has been inoperative for some time. This has resulted in unpredictable sales conditions for corn products, soybeans and meal. The United States is working with Ukraine to establish procedures regarding biotechnology that are based on modern, science-based risk assessment principles and guidelines, including those of the WTO SPS and Technical Barriers to Trade (TBT) Agreements, the Codex Alimentarius, and the International Plant Protection Convention (IPPC).

Fish Shelflife

As part of the bilateral WTO market access agreement with the United States, the Ukrainian government agreed in March 2006 to approve changes to Ukraine's technical regulation on shelflife for fish such as salmon, sardines and roe to bring it into conformity with the CODEX Alimentarius guidelines on the labeling of prepackaged food products and to repeal the previous technical regulation. The government of Ukraine agreed to accept use-by/sell-by dates that are determined solely by the manufacturer.

GOVERNMENT PROCUREMENT

Ukraine is not currently a signatory to the WTO Agreement on Government Procurement (GPA) but will negotiate for membership after it joins the WTO. Ukraine's total government procurement stood at $4.1 billion in 2005 and $3.1 billion for the first half of 2006. Foreign companies generally win only a tiny fraction of the total tenders (0.01 percent during the first half of 2006).

In March 2006, Ukraine promulgated amendments to the law "On Procurement of Goods, Works and Services Using State Funds" of February 22, 2000. The amendments transferred the authority to coordinate government procurement from the Ministry of Economy to the Antimonopoly Committee of Ukraine. The amendments also distributed the authority to oversee government procurement among a range of the governmental agencies, including the Antimonopoly Committee, the Accounting Chamber of Ukraine, and the Tender Chamber of Ukraine. The amendments have been criticized for creating an overlap in authority of various regulatory agencies and decreasing the transparency of the system.

The 2006 amendments also granted the Tender Chamber of Ukraine, a non-governmental organization (NGO), exclusive authority to consider claims of tender participants and issue conclusions. At the same time, this association of public organizations is granted administrative powers characteristic of a state administration agency. The amendments also introduce burdensome and lengthy procurement procedures, and require all tender proposals to be secured by collateral, which limits the number of tender participants and increases the cost of participation.

All government procurement of goods and services valued at more than 2,000 euros and works valued at more than 100,000 euros must be procured through competitive tenders. Open international tenders must be used when procurement is financed by any entity outside of Ukraine. The Tender Chamber of Ukraine publishes information on government procurement in the "State Procurement Bulletin."

Among the problems faced by foreign firms, particularly in smaller procurements, are: (1) the lack of public notice of tender rules and requirements; (2) covert preferences in tender awards; (3) subjecting awards to conditions that were not part of the original tender requirements; and (4) the lack of effective grievance and dispute resolution mechanisms. Although the law prohibits discrimination based on national affiliation, U.S. pharmaceutical companies cite instances where local firms have won government tenders even where the U.S. firms provided the most competitive offer. The law favors local tender participants for purchases of goods not exceeding 200,000 euros, of services not exceeding 300,000 euros, and of works not exceeding 4 million euros. The preference is applied as long as the price differential does not exceed 10 percent. When Ukraine negotiates for membership in WTO Agreement on Government Procurement, many of these issues can be addressed.

Export Barriers

Exports for some categories of products are subject to registration by the Ministry of Economy. Products that must be registered prior to export from Ukraine include: precious metals and stones, rolled metal products exported to the United States, textile products exported to the United States, scrap metal, printer's ink and paper with watermarks. The government has eliminated most export duties, with the prominent exceptions of natural gas, livestock, raw hides, some oil seeds and scrap metal.

Export Restrictions on Grains

Ukraine is the sixth-largest wheat exporter in the world. The United States remains very concerned about the export quotas and licenses that Ukraine imposed on food and feed grain exports beginning at the end of September, 2006. To date, Ukraine has not adequately justified the measures taken, i.e., it has not made the case that it faces a "critical shortage," as required under the General Agreement on Tariffs and Trade of 1994. Several studies point to the contrary. The World Bank's November 2006 report titled "The Quotas on Grain Exports in Ukraine: ineffective, inefficient, and non-transparent" states that the introduction of the quota was not justified, as domestic grain supply was amply adequate to cover all domestic needs. Data from the Food and Agriculture Organization of the United Nations and industry confirm this finding. Further questions are raised by the scope of the measures: the quotas and licenses are being applied to corn and barley, which are not being used for the production of bread in Ukraine, and to corn, barley and wheat used as feedstock.

Meanwhile, the small volumes of licenses that have been issued by the Ukrainian government in late December fall very short of historical trade, especially for wheat. The mismanagement of the issuance of licenses has compounded the problem, leaving a large volume of grain in storage in Ukraine's ports, where in some cases it is deteriorating past the point where it can be used for human consumption, or even animal feedstock.

It is estimated that the costs to grain traders of demurrage and losses from rotting or otherwise compromised grain that has not been able to leave Ukraine's ports will exceed $200 million. The Ukrainian economy is sustaining some of these losses, including lost export opportunities. Ukraine's reputation as a reliable grain exporter, a country that upholds contracts and a good place to invest, is tarnished by these measures. Further, the measures have begun to have a negative impact on Ukraine's farmers themselves, as they have difficulty financing, planning and selling their current and future products.

Live Cattle, Sheep, Hides, and Skins

Export duties have been in place on live cattle, sheep, hides and skins since 1996. For live calves the duty is 75 percent of the customs value (but no less than 1500 euros/ton of live weight); for live cows it is 55 percent (but no less than 540 euros/ton of live weight); and for live sheep it is 50 percent (but no less than 390 euros/ton of live weight). For raw hides of cattle the duty is 30 percent (but no less than 400 euros/ton of live weight); for sheep hides it is 30 percent (but no less than 1 euro/hide); and for pigskins the duty is 27 percent (but no less than 170 euros/ton of live weight). The Ukrainian government has committed to lowering these export duties gradually upon WTO accession.

Scrap Metal

Since January 2003, Ukraine has imposed an export duty of 30 euros/metric ton on ferrous steel scrap and has had, in effect, a ban on exports of non-ferrous metals. The ferrous scrap export duty contributed to a decline in scrap exports from Ukraine, when global demand and prices for steel scrap were rising. Ukrainian metallurgical producers benefited from scrap inputs at prices lower than world levels. As part of its March 2006 bilateral WTO market access agreement with the United States, Ukraine agreed to significantly lower these export duties. Laws passed in the fall of 2006 provide for staged duty reductions to 10 euros/metric ton over a period for six years for ferrous metals and reductions to 15 percent *ad valorem* over a period of five years for non-ferrous metals.

Sunflower Seeds

Sunflower seeds have been subject to an export duty since June 2001, to the benefit of local sunflower oil producers. In July 2005, the export duty on sunflower seeds was lowered to 16 percent of its customs value with further 1 percent annual reductions, to start in 2007, reaching a final duty of 10 percent six years after WTO accession.

INTELLECTUAL PROPERTY RIGHTS (IPR) PROTECTION

The United States withdrew Ukraine's benefits under the Generalized System of Preferences (GSP) program in 2001 and imposed trade sanctions and elevated Ukraine to the Special 301 Priority Watch List in 2002 as a result of Ukraine's record of not protecting intellectual property, such as widespread piracy of copyrighted goods such as compact discs (CDs) and digital video discs (DVDs). The United States lifted sanctions on August 30, 2005, after the Ukrainian government made significant improvements to IPR protection over a number of years, culminating in the passing of amendments to the "Laser-Readable Disk Law" in July 2005. In recognition of Ukraine's efforts to improve the enforcement and protection of intellectual property rights, on January 23, 2006, the United States also reinstated GSP benefits for Ukraine and lowered Ukraine's designation under Special 301 from Priority Foreign Country to Priority Watch List.

Optical Media

The establishment of a regulatory regime for the production, distribution and export/import of optical media several years ago was a major advance. Many of the deficiencies in Ukraine's early laws, which failed to stem the commercial-scale pirate production of CDs, CD-ROMs and DVDs, were addressed by the amendments to the "Laser-Readable Disk Law," which was enacted in July 2005. These new amendments, drafted in close consultation with U.S. industry and the U.S. Government, enhanced law enforcement's role and lowered the threshold for imposing penalties and sanctions. These amendments related to issues such as: (1) establishing a system for monitoring raw materials (optical grade polycarbonate) for optical media production; (2) creating a clear obligation to engrave all manufacturing equipment and molds with SID Codes; (3) expanding non-compliance penalties to include plant closures and deterrent criminal penalties; and (4) stronger enforcement authority to seize infringing machinery and products. Industry recently has identified a problem area with optical disk regulation: alleged counterfeiting of the holograms that legitimate producers are to use, the sale of such holograms on the black market in Ukraine, and their application to pirated CDs and DVDs to circumvent enforcement efforts. The United States has encouraged Ukraine to continue to conduct surprise inspections of optical disc manufacturing facilities, to aggressively prosecute any offenders and shut down pirating plants, and to continue its enforcement efforts at the retail level.

In the first eight months of 2006, the State Department for Intellectual Property (SDIP), the agency responsible for the formulation and implementation of Ukraine's intellectual property laws, and the Ministry of Interior conducted 544 inspections of plants and retail establishments resulting in 101 criminal cases and the seizure of 231,000 units of pirated products valued at more than $1.28 million. All of these numbers exceed the totals for 2005. Furthermore, the Ministry of Internal Affairs, Ministry of Culture, the General Prosecutors' office and the State Security, Tax and Customs Administration have developed a joint program to coordinate their enforcement efforts. In September 2006, Ukraine was notified that it would receive $150,000 in U.S. Government funding to continue efforts to improve prosecution of optical media piracy cases through a grant administered by U.S. Embassy Kyiv, the Ukrainian Ministry of Internal Affairs and SDIP.

Despite the reduction, or near elimination, of illegal production of optical discs, retail sale of copyrighted goods in large markets – especially the notorious Petrivka market – continues to be rampant. Counterfeit hologram stickers complicate enforcement efforts at the retail effort; industry generally regards the hologram sticker system as flawed if not broken. The transit of pirated goods also remains a large problem.

Internet Piracy

In January 2006, the government of Ukraine agreed to work with the U.S. Government and with the U.S. copyright industry to monitor the progress of future enforcement efforts through the Enforcement Cooperation Group (ECG). This bilateral group conducted a successful dialogue in June 2006 that brought additional IPR concerns to Ukraine's attention, particularly the non-transparent operation of copyright royalty collecting societies in Ukraine. In these cases, collecting societies claim to represent performers and rights holders and try to legitimize websites that are allegedly selling pirated music and films. Meanwhile, certain collecting societies have no such arrangements with rights holders or do not remit royalties and fees to them. The United States looks forward to Ukraine amending its Law "On Copyright" to better address the role of collecting societies. The United States continues to monitor the spread of Internet piracy in Ukraine and to work with the Ukrainian government to ensure that its gains on IPR are not reversed. The two governments have agreed to begin joint monitoring of suspected pirate websites.

Business Software

In addition, industry is concerned with growing 'at-source' pre-loaded business software piracy. U.S. industry reports $290 million in losses in Ukraine in 2006 due to business software piracy, and singles out the Ukrainian government as a source of piracy. In June

2006, Microsoft canceled a software legalization agreement with the government of Ukraine due to lack of compliance.

Compliance with Trade-Related Aspects of Intellectual Property Rights (TRIPS)

Ukraine's efforts to accede to the WTO have required it to make some important revisions to its IPR laws. The Rada passed amendments to its Customs Code in November 2006 that provide customs officials the ability to use *ex officio* authority to seize suspected pirated or counterfeit goods. As a result of commitments agreed to as part of its March 2006 WTO bilateral market access agreement with the United States, Ukraine amended its Law "On Medicinal Drugs" to provide a five-year period for the protection of pharmaceutical test data that is submitted to government authorities to obtain marketing approval. This "data exclusivity" protection enters into force in February 2007. The Rada also passed an amendment to the Law "On Pesticides and Agrochemicals" that provides a ten-year period of protection for agricultural chemicals and an amendment to the Law "On Protection of Rights for Indications of Origin of Goods," which sought to improve Ukraine's geographical indications legislation. Further amendments to its legislation related to geographic indications are necessary to bring Ukraine's legislation into full compliance with TRIPS provisions.

Patent and Trademark

The government of Ukraine acknowledges that patent and trademark violations are a problem. Holders of patents or trademarks must often engage with the Ministry of Internal Affairs or the State Customs Service to obtain protection of their rights. Trademarked and copyrighted goods must be registered for a fee ($400 for the first good for the first year; $200 for every next new good; $100 for extension of the registration for the next year) in the Customs Authorities' rights holder database in order to be guaranteed protection. Industry has reported instances of production of counterfeit cigarettes within Ukraine as well as the growth in the amount of counterfeit pesticides and apparel.

The Ukrainian Ministry of Health does not routinely check the validity of patents when it permits pharmaceutical sales in Ukraine. In one case, the Ministry of Health allowed a European company to register the same drug for which a U.S. company held a valid patent. Legal experts and government officials have called for the formation of a special patent court in Ukraine to adjudicate patent cases, but no action has yet been taken to establish the court.

Judicial System

As a result of the low number of judges trained in IPR law and a lack of confidence in the Ukrainian judicial system, civil IPR lawsuits are almost non-existent. The Ukrainian government, however, has brought to court a number of criminal cases related to trademark and copyright violations and the retail sale of pirated goods. The Ministry of Internal Affairs reported that in the first eight months of 2006, 639 crimes in violation of intellectual property rights were detected; of those, 293 were brought to court, and 40 resulted in sentencing of some form, including fines or imprisonment.

SERVICES BARRIERS

Ukraine has few explicit restrictions on services, but they do exist in areas such as insurance, banking activities, auditing, legal services, television and radio broadcasting, and information agencies. As a result of the March 2006 bilateral WTO agreement with the United States, U.S. service providers will benefit from more open access in the areas of energy services, branching in banking and insurance, professional services, express delivery, and telecommunications, among others.

In 2005, the Ukrainian Parliament adopted legislation that will, within five years after WTO accession, permit foreign insurance companies to open branches in Ukraine. In the fall of 2006, it adopted amendments to the law on "Banks and Banking" that would permit foreign banks to open subsidiaries, and adopted a law "On Advocacy" that eliminates the nationality requirements for legal services.

Foreign professionals are permitted to work in Ukraine, but the lack of transparency and the multiplicity of licensing authorities hinder foreign access to the Ukrainian services market. A local content requirement exists for radio and television broadcasting, although it has not been stringently enforced in most cases. Additionally, in January 2006 Ukraine's Parliament adopted a new law on television and radio broadcasting that eliminated restrictions on the share of foreign capital in the charter funds of television and radio broadcasting companies.

U.S. industry identified efforts in Ukraine in 2006 to limit the ability of foreign credit and debit card service providers to provide their services to clients of national electronic payments systems. Ukraine has taken on services commitments in the context of WTO negotiations to maintain an open and competitive banking system, including credit and debit cards, with full market access to electronic payments services. At present, there are no formal restrictions. The United States continues to monitor Ukraine's compliance in this important area.

INVESTMENT BARRIERS

An underdeveloped banking system, poor communications networks, a difficult and frequently changing tax and regulatory climate, crime and corruption, and a weak legal system create obstacles to U.S. investment in Ukraine. The government is working to streamline regulations and eliminate duplicative and confusing laws regarding investment and business. In 2005, Ukraine created several agencies in order to attract investment to Ukraine, including the State Center for Foreign Investment Promotion within the Ministry of Economy, the State Agency for Investment and Innovation, and the State Agency for Investment and Innovation under the President.

The United States has a Bilateral Investment Treaty (BIT) with Ukraine, which took effect in 1996. The BIT guarantees U.S. investors the better of national and MFN treatment, the right to make financial transfers freely and without delay, international legal standards for expropriation and compensation, and access to international arbitration. Despite the BIT, there are a number of longstanding investment disputes faced by several U.S. companies. These disputes mainly date from the early 1990s and the initial opening of the Ukrainian economy to foreign investors. In most cases, however, there has been little progress toward resolution of these cases under subsequent Ukrainian governments.

Taxation

In 2003, Ukraine passed legislation on tax reform, establishing a flat tax on personal income of 13 percent, which will be raised to 15 percent as of January 1, 2007, in accordance with new legislation. In 2003, the Ukrainian government lowered the enterprise profit tax from 27 percent to 25 percent. Arrears in the payment of VAT refunds to exporters has also been a serious problem. Although some improvement in arrears was observed in late 2005 and early 2006, in August 2006, the government of Ukraine decreased the pace of VAT refunds, reimbursing only 76 percent of verified claims, down from 87 percent refunded in 2005. Currently, the process for obtaining a refund of VAT payments can take from 3 to 18 months for foreign companies. In March 2005, the government of Ukraine extended to foreign companies the right to use promissory notes for the payment of VAT on inputs to goods destined for export.

Employees currently pay 3.5 percent of their salaries to state social insurance funds and a 13 percent personal income tax. Additionally, employers pay 38 percent to various state social insurance funds, primarily for pensions. The 2007 draft budget lowers the pension fund tax on salaries by 0.5 percent, but increases payroll tax to the State Pension Fund by 1.4 percent. The 2007 draft budget is heavily criticized for its failure to address payroll deductions to social funds, which is the most burdensome tax. The high payroll taxes are the main reason why shadow wage payments remain common in Ukraine.

Special Economic Zones (SEZs)

Ukraine has in the past maintained two forms of special economic zone (SEZs): Free Economic Zones (FEZs) and Priority Development Territories (PDTs). In April 2005, Ukraine canceled all tax exemptions (i.e., from land tax, corporate income tax, import duty and VAT on imports) to investors in all SEZs to stop large-scale misuse of these zones for tax evasion and smuggling. While the step reduced corruption and expanded the tax base, the abrupt cancellation of privileges and lack of compensatory provisions caused substantial losses to some legitimate investors. Plans to renew tax privileges granted to businesses operating in some SEZs and a compensation mechanism for investors are under consideration by the Ukrainian government. The Ukrainian government also claims that the newly-constituted SEZs will operate in compliance with WTO provisions. On November 15, 2005, the Parliament adopted legislation to create technology parks, providing for some government financial support, targeted subsidies and tax privileges for a list of 16 technoparks based on existing scientific and research institutes.

Privatization

The State Property Fund oversees the privatization process in Ukraine. Privatization rules generally apply to both foreign and domestic investors, and, in theory, a relatively level playing field exists. In contrast to the privatization rush in 2004, few major, new privatizations were conducted in 2005 or 2006. As of October 2006, only 15 percent ($64 million) of this year's target for privatization has been transferred to the budget. Following a difficult reversal of the non-transparent privatization of Ukraine's major steel plant Krivorizhstal, which was subsequently sold in a transparent, well-run tender to Mittal Steel in 2005, the Ukrainian government stated that it had no further plans to reverse previous privatizations.

Ukraine's Parliament amended the Land Code of Ukraine in October 2006, extending a moratorium on the sale of farmland until January 1, 2008. This provision blocks private investors from purchasing some of the 33 million hectares of arable land in Ukraine and will likely constitute a serious obstacle to the development of the agricultural sector.

Corporate Hijacking

Currently, several companies in Ukraine are experiencing an escalation in corporate hijacking activity. These hijackers take advantage of deficient legislation, corrupt courts and a weak regulatory system to gain control of companies at the expense of rightful shareholders. This development harms investors, including U.S. companies and shareholders, and has damaged the image of Ukraine among foreign investors. The Ukrainian government has recognized the seriousness of this problem but has yet to effectively address it.

ELECTRONIC COMMERCE

Electronic commerce is underdeveloped in Ukraine, particularly in the areas outside of Kyiv, where active Internet users number only 7.5 percent of the total population. There is a higher level of usage in Kyiv, where 60 percent of city residents are reportedly active Internet users and where Internet commerce, while small in total volume, is experiencing strong annual growth. Many of the elements needed for thriving electronic commerce, such as high consumer demand for goods and services, capable software engineers to design websites and availability of credit cards are present in Ukraine. However, the low levels of usage, limited services by retailers and a general distrust among the population prevent electronic commerce from gaining popularity. The more than 100 Internet retailers that exist in Ukraine are almost entirely based in Kyiv. Most Ukrainian Internet retailer sites consist of price lists or advertising with an option to place an order that later could be delivered after a cash payment, card payment or bank transfer is received. In some instances, Internet shops accept online payments from clients of their partner banks only. The main products sold via the Internet are home appliances and electronics, especially mobile phones, while the main services include Internet banking and online bill payment for utilities.

In 2003, the Ukrainian parliament adopted three laws regulating the Internet and establishing a framework for the telecommunications market. The National Council on Communications is entrusted with monitoring the telecommunications market. The Internet in Ukraine remains mostly unregulated. In April 2005, the Ministry of Transport and Communication introduced a controversial regulation forcing registration of Internet websites in Ukraine. The law was cancelled in October 2005, however, after a public outcry labeled the measure a violation of freedom of speech and expression.

OTHER BARRIERS

Problematic Legal Framework

A sound legal system and properly running judiciary system are critical for sustainable economic growth, reducing the cost and risk of doing business, and attracting FDI. Unfortunately, the Commercial and Civil Codes, a foundation for the entire legal system in Ukraine, are full of discrepancies and conflicting provisions. Both codes became effective in January 2004, but their approaches to the regulation of business activities (i.e., issues related to regulation of bank accounts, securities, contracts, etc.) are contradictory. The Commercial Code has a number of provisions considered to be incompatible with market economics, and most experts believe it should be eliminated entirely.

Inspections

The frequency of inspections by regulatory agencies is one of the major hindrances to business development in Ukraine. The annual number of inspections conducted throughout the country exceeds 1.5 million. According to a recent study, 57 percent of the private businesses in Ukraine consider inspections to be unclear, complicated and non-transparent. Ukraine's system of inspections does not fulfill its main purpose of preventing legal abuses, but is primarily punitive in nature.

Chapter 8

UZBEKISTAN

TRADE SUMMARY

The U.S. goods trade deficit with Uzbekistan was $97 million in 2006, an increase of $76 million from $22 million in 2005. U.S. goods exports in 2006 were $54 million, down 26.9 percent from the previous year. Corresponding U.S. imports from Uzbekistan were $151 million, up 58.4 percent. Uzbekistan is currently the 148th largest export market for U.S. goods.

The stock of U.S. foreign direct investment in Uzbekistan in 2005 was $114 million (latest data available), up from $107 million in 2004.

The U.S.-Uzbekistan Bilateral Trade Agreement, which entered into force in 1994, provides for normal trade relations (NTR) between the United States and Uzbekistan and governs other aspects of the bilateral trade relationship. The U.S. Government, however, has not acted to bring this agreement into force, and is unlikely to do so until the investment climate in Uzbekistan significantly improves. In 2004, the Uzbeks signed the regional Trade Investment Framework Agreement (TIFA) with the U.S. Trade Representative's Office and its four Central Asian neighbors. Uzbekistan is still negotiating terms of accession to the World Trade Organization (WTO).

IMPORT POLICIES

The government of Uzbekistan restricts imports in many ways, including through high import duties, licensing requirements for importers and wholesale traders, restricted access for sellers of imported items to retail space, and limited access to hard currency and the local currency (the soum).

Uzbekistan's trade policy is based on import substitution. The multiple exchange rate system and the highly over-regulated trade regime have led to both import and export declines since 1996, although imports have declined more than exports, as the government squeezed imports to maintain hard currency reserves. Draconian tariffs, sporadic border closures and crossing "fees" decrease imports of both consumer products and capital equipment.

Highly discriminatory excise taxes exist to protect locally-produced goods. Unofficial payments to customs officials are a normal part of trans-border trade. Imports are prohibitively expensive for the majority of Uzbeks, due to duties on products such as cars, electronics, appliances, foodstuffs and textiles. The government claims the duties are a temporary measure to prevent a surge in imports while it gradually eliminates barriers to trade, such as hard currency quotas, as part of the economic reform process.

Excise tax, charged as a percentage of the declared customs value, must be paid on certain products, such as cigarettes, vodka, ice-cream, oil and gas condensate, fuels, cars and carpets. Excise tax rates vary depending on the type of imported good and may deviate significantly. In 2005, the government raised excise taxes between 30 percent and 70 percent on a number of meat products. On December 18, 2006, new excise taxes were introduced for basic consumer items, varying from 5 percent to 200 percent depending on local production of like goods. In 2006, excise taxes accounted for approximately 12.6 percent of the total Uzbek budget revenue. The U.S. Embassy estimates the average increase in excise taxes for 2007 is 15 percent.

According to reports from foreign investors, "unofficial duties" combined with other tariffs and taxes can cost as much as 100 percent to 150 percent of the amount of the actual value of the product, making the product unaffordable for virtually everyone in the country. For example, imported liquor is subject to an excise tax of 70 percent to 85 percent (depending on type) versus 40 percent to 65 percent for domestic liquors. Additionally, at the retail level, imported automobiles have been subjected to duties and taxes totaling approximately 100 percent. Tariffs are officially 30 percent for most textile products, home furnishings and essentially all other fabrics and apparel, and 90 percent for carpets and rugs.

The government also requires retailers to present certificates of origin and customs receipts for imported products upon the request of tax or customs authorities. The Uzbek government often confiscates goods found without such certificates. A decree enacted in August 2004 imposed further bureaucratic restrictions on traders. In addition to demanding that all individual traders be registered with the local authorities and the Ministry for Foreign Economic Relations, Investment and Trade, traders will have to prove that they have a commercial bank account and imported the goods themselves from the originating country. Surveys of foreign companies consistently conclude that restrictions on access to local currency in order to transact business and pay employees is one of the worst of the many serious obstacles to doing business in Uzbekistan.

In 2005 and 2006 the Uzbekistan government continued to restrict imports by limiting access to hard currency for private importers. Uzbekistan introduced currency convertibility in October 2003. Although the government committed itself to the provisions of IMF's Article VIII on currency convertibility, multiple restrictions remain in place. All legal entities, including those with foreign investments, must have the Central Bank's permission to deal in foreign currency.

The government continues to restrict consumer goods imports in order to prevent hard currency flows and curb the threat of devaluation of the soum. In both 2005 and 2006, private businesses reported regular conversion delays of three months from August through December.

Although clearance of import contracts with the state-controlled clearing company is no longer needed for customs registration, the regulation requiring the registration has not been abolished. The State Customs Committee still turns down about 5 percent of contracts submitted for registration, purportedly due to mistakes in documents. The companies entitled to convert local currency under import contracts encounter problems with arbitrary requests for documentation by banks. While the required documents are outlined in the instructions issued by the relevant bank, these instructions are often amended without any prior notice. As a result, documents are often rejected on disputable grounds and conversion can be delayed, which results in devaluation losses for the importer. Businesses must deposit the funds to be converted with the Central Bank for the entire duration of the Committee's review of the request. Bank dealers have reported cases in which the Central Bank did not approve applications for conversion for some of their clients who needed large sums of hard currency.

In addition to official barriers, the customs clearance process is overburdened with unofficial bureaucratic obstacles leading to significant processing delays of two to three months, even for U.S.-Uzbek joint ventures. Problems include the arbitrary seizure of goods, as well as frequent official and unofficial changes in customs procedures without prior notification. Excessive documentation also makes the Uzbek importing process costly and time consuming. The lack of proper equipment and legislative regulations creates an environment in which the customs official on duty can arbitrarily apply his or her own case-by-case search and seizure procedures. In 2004, the government of Uzbekistan made an effort to increase the transparency of regulations used at customs border posts, primarily by posting all relevant regulations and decrees where traders can review them.

Surveys of foreign companies consistently conclude that trade/border/customs restrictions are the worst of many serious obstacles to doing business in Uzbekistan. Despite the fact that there is a law legalizing duty-free imports for foreign investors, it is mandatory to have a legally binding agreement with the government that waives customs fees and other duties when importing goods for investment purposes.

STANDARDS, TESTING, LABELING AND CERTIFICATION

The system of standardization, accreditation, certification and application of sanitary and phytosanitary (SPS) standards presents significant barriers to trade. Uzbekistan accepts U.S. manufacturers' self-certification of conformity with Uzbek foreign product standards and environmental regulations. All foreign products must be labeled in Russian and Uzbek. Domestic entities, including government enterprises, must also meet these mandatory-labeling requirements. The National Agency of Standards (Uzstandard) is in charge of certification and accreditation. The government is still in the process of drafting a new law on technical regulations.

In August 2004, Uzbekistan's Parliament ratified a decision to join the International Union on Plants Variety Protection, which has been in force since November 11, 2004.

GOVERNMENT PROCUREMENT

There is no systematic approach to government procurement in Uzbekistan. Instead, procurement decisions are generally made on a decentralized and *ad hoc* basis. Often, the procurement practices of the central government are similar to those of many countries, incorporating tenders, bid documents, bids and a formal contract award. A law enacted in 2002 created more transparency in the procurement process by mandating that all government procurement over $100,000 be completed on a tender basis. However, many tenders are announced with short deadlines and are awarded to companies in a non-transparent manner. Uzbekistan is in the process of modifying its trade regime to become a member of the WTO, and it is not yet a signatory of the WTO Agreement on Government Procurement. However, government entities are more frequently announcing tenders in local newspapers and magazines.

The most serious barrier to trade with respect to government procurement is in the field of contract obligations. There are numerous cases in which the Uzbek government is not complying with contract obligations in relation to procuring equipment, equipment pricing and payment guarantees. Further, there are several cases in which a U.S. company provided product for a government tender and then was not paid.

EXPORT SUBSIDIES

The government of Uzbekistan provides agricultural subsidies on cotton in the form of heavily subsidized inputs, such as electricity, water and fertilizer, to farmers who can then sell their cotton directly to the government. This creates an end product that can be sold more cheaply in the international market. Moreover, in December 2002, the government issued regulations allowing cotton farmers to sell half of their actual harvest, most often to the government, at more favorable prices than those allowed in the state order system. It is unclear, however, how well the new regulation is being enforced by the end consumer, which in 90 percent of cases is still the Uzbek government.

INTELLECTUAL PROPERTY RIGHTS (IPR) PROTECTION

Significant deficiencies remain in Uzbekistan's intellectual property protection regime. Due to these deficiencies, there is an ongoing review of Uzbekistan's status as a beneficiary country under the U.S. Generalized System of Preferences (GSP) Program. Uzbekistan has been on the Special 301 Watch List since 2000.

The government adopted the "Law on Copyright and Related Rights" in 2006. The law provides comprehensive definitions of terms, addresses collective rights management and compulsory licensing to the producers of phonograms, authors, performers and subjects of related rights. In 2005, Uzbekistan joined the Berne Convention for the Protection of Literary and Artistic Works (Berne Convention), but the government declared an exception to Article 18, which requires that signatory countries extend copyright protection to pre-existing works.

It is a challenge to purchase legal recordings in Uzbekistan. Current border enforcement is weak. As a result, illegal recordings freely cross into Uzbekistan for sale. Additional personnel and training courses are needed for more effective border enforcement. Uzbekistan does not provide for either civil or criminal *ex parte* search procedures needed for effective anti-piracy enforcement.

SERVICES BARRIERS

The government has created an insurance supervisory board and a licensing system for insurance companies. Uzbekistan imposes a 10 percent withholding tax on reinsurance premiums for policies with reinsurers from countries that do not have a double taxation treaty with Uzbekistan. As the United States and Uzbekistan do not have such a treaty, U.S. reinsurers must add the 10 percent charge to their premiums.

Uzbek law grants state-owned companies a monopoly over certain forms of mandatory state insurance (i.e., mandatory insurance paid for out of the state budget). Foreign banks may not operate in Uzbekistan except in a subsidiary status, which makes the banks subject to Uzbek laws, including the requirement of a charter capitalization fund of $20 million. This is a common requirement in other Commonwealth of Independent States (CIS) countries as well. The $20 million fund requirement does not apply to Uzbek firms. The government determines the required size of the charter funds for Uzbek firms on a case-bycase basis.

The government has granted exclusive control over all international telecommunications services to the Uzbektelekom Company, the largest national telecommunications operator owned by the state. All international voice and data transmission services, including Internet and IP-telephony, must be provided over Uzbektelekom's network. All national data transmission services must be provided by UZNET, a branch of Uzbektelecom.

INVESTMENT BARRIERS

According to official statistics, foreign investment for the first nine months of 2006 totaled $545.9 million. However, the Uzbeks classify foreign loans for goods and services as foreign investment. Uzbekistan says it plans to attract $1.22 billion dollars of foreign investment in 2007.

Under two laws implemented in 1998, to be considered "an enterprise with foreign investment" a firm must be at least 30 percent foreign-owned and have initial foreign equity of $150,000; otherwise, a firm is treated as a domestic enterprise. Normally this equity is "hidden" through assets such as equipment or technical expertise. Although reduced from previous levels, these ownership and capital requirements are still high enough to discourage foreign investment by small companies. U.S.-owned companies in Uzbekistan also face cumbersome regulations and licensing requirements. Profit repatriation remains extremely difficult for foreign-owned companies due to frequent government interference and restrictions on currency conversion.

In the past, businesses wishing to initiate operations in Uzbekistan were required to register and obtain licenses from several different government entities. In 2001, the government introduced legislation to create a "one-stop shop" to make the registration process easier. These one-stop shops, which are located in local government offices (hokimiyats) throughout Uzbekistan, have reportedly made it easier to start a new business. But even with the new regulations, businesses often must satisfy bureaucratic requirements in multiple government offices.

Uzbekistan's Tax Code, introduced for the first time in 1998, lacks provisions that are key parts of the tax regime in most countries. For example, unless a company receives permission through a special presidential decree, Uzbekistan allows no credit for VAT on capital imports, including plant, machinery, and buildings. This practice puts firms operating in Uzbekistan at a competitive disadvantage compared to those in countries that do allow such credits. In addition, earnings of foreign-owned enterprises are subject to double taxation.

Another significant problem in the Uzbek Tax Code relates to the classification of expenses. Many expenses that are normally deductible for purposes of calculating taxable profits are not deductible under the Tax Code, thereby increasing the effective tax burden in comparison to other countries. In most countries, for example, expenses such as advertising and business travel are not subject to taxation. In Uzbekistan, however, travel is not deductible and the deductibility of advertising is linked to an archaic and onerous formula. In 2005, the government initiated a major revision of the tax code. The changes, however, have yet to be officially announced or implemented. The government continues to work with local tax experts and the United Nations Development Program to complete its revision of the tax code.

Foreign firms in Uzbekistan face higher than average labor costs. The corporate income tax rate has been lowered to 10 percent over the past two years, but firms must also make a mandatory contribution for insurance of 24 percent. While most Uzbek companies evade their tax obligations, foreign investors generally adhere to the law. U.S. companies have also complained that Uzbek laws are not interpreted or applied in a consistent manner. On many occasions, local officials have interpreted laws in a manner that is harmful to individual private investors or to the business community more broadly. Companies are particularly concerned about the lack of consistency and fairness in the application of the Foreign Investment Law, which contains a number of specific protections for foreign investors.

Due to the burdensome, unstable tax and regulatory environment, foreign investors in Uzbekistan often seek special tax and regulatory abatements in the form of Cabinet of Ministers decrees, which must be signed by the President in order to be approved. Such decrees have been helpful to foreign investors in certain strategic industries (e.g., mining, oil and gas, and large manufacturing). The process of requesting tax or regulatory abatements is lengthy and unpredictable, however, and lacks the necessary transparency required to attract significant investment over the longer term. Despite the protections that such decrees are meant to provide, investors working under Cabinet of Ministers decrees still face significant regulatory and bureaucratic impediments.

Persons doing business in Uzbekistan note that if they are engaged in a sector in which either the government or an Uzbek-controlled firm is a competitor, they face higher bureaucratic hurdles and currency conversion problems. Potential competitors are often not allowed to invest in such sectors. The regulatory framework for joint ventures in Uzbekistan is extremely burdensome. Many international corporations complain that the government demands more financial reports than are necessary from shareholders.

The judiciary in Uzbekistan is not independent. In the event of disputes, courts usually favor firms that are controlled or owned by the state. Disputes involving foreign-owned businesses are common and have proven difficult to resolve even with high-level intervention from senior U.S. officials.

Investors cannot count on the government to honor an international arbitration award in favor of a foreign plaintiff. A late 2006 government court reinterpretation of Uzbek arbitration regulations states that unless both Uzbek and foreign partners agree in writing to conduct a specific arbitration, the government will not honor an arbitral award. Contractual provisions for international arbitration are insufficient. If international arbitration is permitted, awards can be challenged in domestic courts. The Ministry of Justice is responsible for the resolution of all international commercial disputes, but the Ministry's power is limited and frequently co-opted by more influential powers within the government. A number of foreign companies have not received full payment even after being awarded monetary damages in international arbitration. Others have pursued claims and won in the Uzbek courts, only to have the government refuse to enforce the award. There are several cases, however, in which international arbitration awards have been successfully enforced.

Another barrier to investment is the perception that Uzbekistan will not consistently implement its international obligations. One long-standing case involves a decision in favor of an international grain company by the Grain and Feed Trade Association in London, the arbiter agreed to by Uzbekistan when the contract was signed. Uzbekistan has indicated that it will not honor the arbitral award.

OTHER BARRIERS

Much of the Soviet-era economic system remains today, needlessly complicating simple transactions and costing businesses time and money to overcome. Uzbekistan's extensive trade barriers encourage consumers to buy domestically-produced goods. High duties, taxes and tariffs price the majority of imported consumer goods out of reach for the average Uzbek who earns $50-80/month. Corruption at all levels of government creates non-transparent, often kleptocratic, tender processes. Local enforcement of international and domestic rule of law is unreliable; special decrees for business tax benefits can be, and are, capriciously revoked. With so many overlapping, and somewhat intangible trade barriers, it is difficult to gauge the specific monetary impact a barrier has on the U.S.-Uzbek trade balance. The removal, or softening, of one barrier would likely cause another's augmentation, if not the creation of an entirely new barrier. The overall poor political climate between the United States and Uzbekistan has also been a formidable barrier to trade.

American investors unanimously complain that they do not control their corporate bank accounts in Uzbekistan. The main problem involves restrictions on businesses' access to, and use of, cash in their accounts. Every routine banking operation requires official permission. As a result, businesses expend an enormous amount of senior staff time on simple transactions. A March 24, 2000, decree improved this situation by allowing many farms, restaurants, cafes and other small and medium enterprises with foreign investment ($150,000 or more in foreign capital) to access their own funds in commercial bank accounts, so long as those funds were received and deposited within the previous 90 days.

Most other businesses may hold cash for only a small number of permitted purposes, such as paying salaries and travel expenses. All other money must be held in the bank. Cash receipts must be deposited on the day in which they are received. Even small purchases, such as office supplies, must be paid for using a bank transfer. Uzbek companies handle this problem by making salary withdrawals for nonexistent staff. Western accounting practices prevent U.S. companies from using these deceptive practices, and instead, companies are required to wait for as long as a week or more for a wire transfer to arrive before purchases of any kind can be made.

Local and international entrepreneurs face payoff-seeking officials due to pervasive corruption, exacerbated by low salaries for officials and an opaque, cumbersome, and internally contradictory legal regime that makes it difficult for business owners to comply with Uzbek regulations. It is reported that local, regional, and national officials, police officers, as well as tax, customs, fire, health, safety, and labor inspectors are all susceptible to bribery and other corrupt practices.

INDEX

A

access, 2, 6, 12, 43, 44, 45, 47, 48, 49, 50, 63, 70, 71, 73, 75, 77, 79, 80, 81, 91, 96, 101, 102, 103, 105, 115, 118, 125, 126, 129, 130, 135
accidents, 104
accountability, 14, 68
accounting, 47, 93, 135
accounting standards, 93
accreditation, 54, 131
acquis communautaire, 54
acquisitions, 51, 75
adaptation, 11, 37
advertisements, 39, 73
advertising, 27, 42, 77, 127, 134
advisory body, 8
aerosols, 27
aerospace, 30, 32
Africa, 6, 59
age, 86
agent, 60, 72, 101
aging, 95
agricultural exports, 2, 100
agricultural sector, 17, 19, 59, 69, 70, 99, 127
agriculture, vii, 15, 60, 70, 79, 99, 108, 115
air carriers, 57
airlines, 81, 95, 104
Alaska, 4
alcohol, 41, 76, 81, 82, 83, 117
alternative(s), 8, 9, 13, 16, 24, 25, 42, 67, 77, 92
aluminum, 4, 60
ambiguity, 46, 58
amendments, 4, 21, 39, 40, 88, 90, 95, 116, 118, 120, 122, 124, 125
animals, 4, 21, 22, 24, 71, 72, 117
apparel, 40, 63, 110, 124, 130
arbitration, 10, 67, 111, 112, 126, 134
Argentina, 20, 57
arrest, 64
assessment, 2, 9, 14, 15, 20, 85, 119
assessment procedures, 85, 119
assets, 76, 94, 95, 104, 133
attacks, 15
attention, 74, 123
Attorney General, 64, 68
auditing, 47, 125
Australia, 51
Austria, 6, 15, 16, 17, 28, 29, 42, 45, 47, 48, 49, 53
authentication, 97
authority, 12, 15, 31, 39, 55, 64, 82, 90, 92, 94, 102, 103, 105, 111, 120, 122, 124
automobiles, 24, 81, 113, 117, 130
availability, 29, 127
awareness, 64

B

Balkans, 38
bandwidth, 65
bank ownership, 75
banking, 52, 53, 56, 79, 91, 99, 104, 107, 125, 127, 135
bankruptcy, 30
banks, 53, 56, 91, 127, 131, 133
barley, 4, 121
barriers, vii, 1, 2, 4, 7, 13, 20, 23, 45, 52, 54, 59, 69, 70, 79, 80, 82, 92, 104, 130, 131, 135
barriers to entry, 54
batteries, 26, 64
beef, 2, 4, 13, 21, 71, 80, 85, 86, 100, 107, 117, 118, 119
behavior, 18, 105
Belgium, 7, 33, 38, 44
beverages, 72, 80, 107, 108, 117
bias, 29
binding, 25, 26, 32, 57, 88, 111, 131

biofuel, 17
biosafety, 86
biotechnology, 13, 14, 15, 16, 17, 18, 19, 20, 61, 69, 72, 85, 86, 87, 99, 100, 101, 119
black market, 123
blocks, 76, 127
board members, 30, 95
bonds, 68
border control, 22, 100
bovine spongiform encephalopathy, 86, 119
branching, 91, 125
Brazil, 42
breakfast, 71
breeding, 108
bribes, 66, 68, 112
broadband, 49, 50, 52, 75, 102
buffer, 7, 55
buildings, 63, 134
Bulgaria, 2, 3, 4, 7, 20, 22, 28, 36, 38, 53
Bureau of Customs and Border Protection, 57
bureaucracy, 111
by-products, 21, 85, 86

C

cable service, 41
cadmium, 25, 26
call centers, 65
campaigns, 14
Canada, 1, 42, 57
capital controls, 52
capital expenditure, 95
capital flows, 96
carbohydrate, 71
Caribbean, 6
categorization, 8
cattle, 21, 86, 108, 121
CE, 19, 26, 108
cell, 49, 66
Central Asia, 129
certainty, 26
certificate, 62, 66, 81, 85, 87, 100, 108, 117, 119
certification, 15, 23, 28, 59, 61, 79, 84, 85, 87, 92, 117, 118, 131
channels, 39
China, 97
chromium, 25
citizenship, 104
civil servants, 8
civil society, 68
classes, 10, 54
classification, 2, 3, 84, 134
clients, 45, 125, 127, 131

climate change, 27, 28
closure, 110
cluster bomb, 76
CO2, 78
coal, 60, 95
codes, 66, 93, 128
coffee, 60, 87
coke, 60
collateral, 120
colleges, 54
commerce, 90, 96, 97, 127
commercial bank, 130, 135
commercials, 40
commodity(ies), 2, 3, 4, 70, 71, 85, 87, 101, 109
common external tariff, 3, 59
Common Market, 59
Commonwealth of Independent States, 133
communication, 4, 65
community, 18, 27, 35, 53, 58, 62, 103, 134
comparative advantage, vii
compensation, 3, 17, 42, 44, 71, 73, 93, 126
compensation package, 42
competence, 52
competition, 8, 30, 31, 44, 45, 48, 49, 50, 51, 62, 66, 67, 70, 71, 75, 102, 103, 104, 110
competitive process, 32
competitiveness, 32, 35
competitor, 50, 83, 134
complement, 62
complexity, 31
compliance, 6, 21, 37, 81, 84, 88, 110, 115, 117, 119, 122, 124, 125, 126
components, 36
composition, 16, 23
compounds, 10, 28
computer software, 73
computers, 4
concentrates, 4
concentration, 22, 25
concrete, 37
conditioning, 26, 27, 28
confidence, 67
conflict, 63
conformity, 14, 61, 64, 84, 85, 108, 117, 118, 119, 131
confusion, 30, 68, 110
Congress, iv, 81
consensus, 18, 103
consolidation, 42, 96
constraints, 61
construction, 30, 33, 35, 54, 83, 84, 95
consumer goods, 79, 88, 118, 130, 135
consumer protection, 118

consumers, 1, 10, 12, 17, 57, 60, 66, 72, 77, 83, 96, 135
consumption, 21, 71, 88, 97, 108, 113, 121
control, 7, 16, 59, 67, 71, 76, 88, 95, 96, 108, 113, 127, 133, 135
conversion, 130, 131, 133, 134
copper, 84
corn, 2, 4, 18, 19, 20, 59, 99, 119, 121
corporate governance, 53, 111, 113
corporations, 62, 67, 134
corruption, 30, 31, 62, 66, 68, 76, 93, 125, 126, 136
cosmetics, 24, 83, 110
costs, 6, 7, 13, 24, 27, 32, 33, 47, 48, 61, 62, 66, 68, 71, 77, 82, 103, 108, 121, 134
cotton, 60, 132
Council of Europe, 47
Council of Ministers, 15, 26, 52, 54
counter-trade, 29
country of origin, 43, 57, 61, 100
Court of Appeals, 49
coverage, 4, 71, 85
covering, 29, 48, 79
CPC, 95
credibility, 67
credit, 91, 125, 127, 134
creditors, 112
crime, 41, 74, 125
criminal activity, 30
critical infrastructure, 55
criticism, 95
crop production, 18
crops, 15, 16, 17, 18, 19, 20, 61, 101
cultivation, 20
culture, vii
currency, vii, 96, 129, 130, 131, 133, 134
customers, 50, 51, 105
customs issues, 82
Customs Service, 116, 124
Customs Union, 59, 110
Cyprus, 7, 17, 39, 42, 53, 54
Czech Republic, 8, 29, 30, 39, 42, 45

D

data communication, 65
data processing, 4, 91, 107
database, 24, 124
debt, 11, 32
decision-making process, 9
decisions, 2, 8, 11, 25, 31, 48, 49, 62, 70, 77, 82, 116, 131
defendants, 39, 42
defense, 29, 30, 31, 32, 55, 73, 87, 93, 96, 118

deficiency, 66, 86
definition, 43, 109
delivery, 15, 44, 72, 91, 96, 103, 125
demand, 19, 38, 43, 59, 95, 127
Denmark, 8, 16, 28, 48, 49, 53, 77
Department of Agriculture, 86
Department of Commerce, 57
depreciation, 112
desire, 103
destruction, 16, 18, 65, 83, 90
detergents, 64
devaluation, 130, 131
development assistance, 34
diesel fuel, 116
direct investment, 111
directives, 14, 16, 48, 49, 52, 72, 76, 78, 109
discipline, 34
disclosure, 35, 39, 70, 113
discrimination, 76, 120
discs, 38, 41, 60, 122, 123
displacement, 78, 81
dissatisfaction, 100
distortions, 7, 84
distribution, 6, 7, 18, 29, 39, 42, 65, 67, 76, 88, 90, 91, 93, 94, 103, 105, 112, 122
diversity, 103
division, 52
doctors, 7, 9, 11, 54, 111
Doha Development Agenda, 3,
Doha Development Round, 70
domestic demand, 88
dominance, 9
donors, 62, 68
doors, 36
draft, 4, 9, 13, 17, 22, 28, 44, 53, 55, 61, 87, 94, 96, 111, 126
drinking water, 29
drugs, 6, 7, 8, 9, 10, 11, 12, 36, 64, 77, 80
DSL, 51
dual-use items, 55
Duma, 81, 83, 85, 88, 89, 94, 96
duration, 110, 131
duties, vii, 4, 21, 35, 59, 60, 63, 71, 74, 81, 82, 84, 93, 94, 100, 107, 116, 117, 120, 121, 122, 129, 130, 131, 135
duty-free treatment, 4

E

earnings, 134
East Asia, 63
Eastern Europe, 10
economic efficiency, vii

economic growth, 111
economic integration, 1
economic reform, 130
Ecuador, 5, 6
education, 54
EEA, 47, 53, 69, 71, 72, 75, 76
electrical power, 93
electricity, 76, 105, 112, 132
electronic communications, 48
electronic trade, 96
embargo, 16
emission, 27
employees, 30, 55, 68, 77, 130
employment, 68, 70
encryption, 80, 94, 97, 117
energy, 26, 29, 55, 79, 83, 84, 90, 91, 94, 95, 105, 112, 125
energy efficiency, 26, 84
England, 46
enlargement, 2, 3, 4
entrepreneurs, 136
environment, 8, 9, 24, 25, 26, 49, 50, 61, 86, 111, 131, 134
environmental protection, 70
environmental regulations, 131
environmental standards, 67
equipment, 14, 25, 26, 27, 28, 29, 30, 31, 33, 39, 55, 58, 60, 63, 80, 83, 84, 90, 94, 107, 117, 118, 122, 129, 131, 132, 133
equity, 32, 54, 55, 67, 75, 76, 91, 111, 133
Estonia, 17, 42
estradiol, 21
ethers, 25
ethyl alcohol, 81
EU, vii, 1, 2, 3, 4, 5, 6, 7, 8, 9, 10, 11, 13, 14, 15, 16, 17, 18, 19, 20, 21, 22, 23, 24, 25, 26, 27, 28, 29, 30, 31, 32, 34, 35, 36, 37, 38, 39, 40, 41, 42, 43, 44, 45, 46, 47, 48, 49, 50, 51, 52, 53, 54, 55, 56, 57, 69, 71, 72, 73, 74, 75, 76, 77, 91, 100, 101, 104, 107, 108, 109, 110
Europe, i, iii, 7, 14, 20, 40, 49, 79, 84, 108
European Commission, 2, 3, 8, 10, 13, 14, 15, 16, 18, 21, 22, 23, 24, 25, 26, 34, 35, 36, 37, 42, 43, 44, 47, 48, 50, 52, 57
European Community, 14, 24, 37, 47
European Court of Justice, 15, 37
European Parliament, 26, 43, 44, 53
European Union, v, vii, 1, 2, 3, 4, 5, 6, 15, 20, 23, 25, 27, 37, 42, 44, 45, 62, 69, 84, 100, 104, 110
examinations, 46
exchange rate, 10, 129
exclusion, 15
exercise, 66

expertise, 90, 133
exploitation, 53
exporter, 94, 121
exports, 1, 2, 4, 6, 7, 13, 14, 16, 20, 21, 22, 23, 34, 59, 60, 63, 69, 79, 81, 82, 84, 86, 94, 97, 99, 100, 107, 109, 115, 116, 117, 118, 119, 121, 129
extraction, 95

F

failure, 14, 35, 51, 57, 89, 126
fairness, 9, 134
family, 73
Far East, 97
farmers, 17, 18, 19, 70, 121, 132
farmland, 127
farms, 135
FDI, 1, 69, 79, 99, 107, 115, 128
fear(s), 26, 64, 92
Federal Communications Commission, 102
federal government, 33, 101, 104
federal law, 87, 91, 93
film(s), 43, 44, 64, 88, 103, 110, 123
finance, 1, 26, 66, 103
financial institutions, 67, 75
financial support, 126
financial system, 96
financing, 9, 25, 32, 63, 121
Finland, 8, 22, 28, 42, 45, 48, 49
firms, 1, 8, 9, 10, 11, 29, 30, 31, 45, 46, 47, 52, 53, 55, 56, 58, 61, 62, 63, 65, 66, 67, 68, 69, 76, 77, 83, 88, 90, 91, 95, 99, 101, 104, 112, 120, 133, 134
fish, 4, 71, 84, 116, 119
fishing, 67
flame, 25
flexibility, 26, 27, 43, 57
flow of capital, 96
fluctuations, 59
foams, 27, 28
food, 4, 15, 16, 18, 21, 23, 38, 61, 70, 71, 72, 79, 80, 81, 82, 83, 84, 87, 107, 119, 121
food processing industry, 70, 71
food products, 16, 23, 61, 70, 71, 80, 87, 119
food safety, 15, 16
footwear, 27, 40
foreign banks, 91, 125
foreign direct investment, 1, 52, 59, 68, 69, 79, 99, 107, 109, 111, 115, 129
foreign firms, 66, 102, 120
foreign investment, 54, 56, 67, 75, 76, 92, 93, 94, 104, 130, 133, 135
forests, 75

forgiveness, 32
France, 8, 17, 18, 23, 30, 32, 33, 34, 39, 43, 45, 47, 48, 49, 53, 54, 55, 102
fraud, 30, 34, 94
free trade, vii
free trade area, vii
freedom, 46, 128
freezing, 85
friction, 44
friends, 73
fructose, 4, 111
fruits, 4, 107
frustration, 2, 14
fuel, 13, 60, 83
funding, 62, 79, 115, 123
funds, 6, 31, 33, 63, 73, 93, 125, 126, 131, 133, 135
furniture, 87

G

gambling, 54
gases, 27, 28
gasoline, 116
GATS, 42, 47, 52
GATT, 2, 3, 4, 5, 38, 116
GDP, 70, 76
General Agreement on Tariffs and Trade, 2, 3, 121
General Agreement on Trade in Services, 42
Generalized System of Preferences, 70, 88, 122, 132
generation, 95, 102
generic drugs, 10
Germany, 9, 16, 18, 32, 34, 39, 40, 44, 46, 48, 49, 53, 55
glass, 60
global competition, 70
global demand, 121
glucose, 71
goals, 72
goods and services, 29, 31, 55, 76, 120, 127, 133
governance, 41, 113
government, vii, 1, 6, 7, 8, 9, 10, 11, 12, 15, 16, 17, 18, 19, 20, 28, 29, 30, 31, 32, 33, 34, 36, 38, 39, 40, 41, 42, 44, 47, 48, 50, 51, 54, 55, 58, 59, 60, 61, 62, 63, 64, 65, 66, 67, 68, 69, 72, 73, 75, 76, 77, 78, 79, 80, 81, 82, 83, 84, 85, 86, 87, 88, 89, 90, 91, 92, 93, 94, 95, 96, 97, 99, 100, 101, 102, 103, 105, 107, 108, 111, 112, 113, 115, 117, 119, 120, 121, 122, 123, 124, 125, 126, 127, 129, 130, 131, 132, 133, 134, 135
government budget, 73, 81
government expenditure, 12
government policy, vii, 111

government procurement, 7, 29, 30, 73, 87, 101, 119, 120, 131, 132
GPA, 28, 29, 73, 101, 119
grains, 70, 107, 116
grants, 33, 34, 39, 64, 69, 71, 73, 75, 81, 133
grasses, 17
Greece, 18, 23, 28, 30, 38, 40, 47, 48, 55, 56
greed, 1, 26
greenhouse gases, 27
grouping, 48
groups, 9, 19, 39, 73, 75
growth, 11, 21, 35, 65, 71, 94, 96, 100, 119, 124, 127
growth hormone, 21, 71, 100
guidance, 12, 16, 25, 26
guidelines, 12, 61, 65, 76, 85, 90, 109, 119

H

hands, 76
hard currency, 129, 130, 131
harm, 90, 107
harmonization, 26, 48, 100
hazardous wastes, 80
health, vii, 2, 7, 8, 9, 10, 11, 12, 15, 16, 23, 24, 55, 58, 60, 62, 77, 93, 100, 113, 118, 136
health care, 2, 7, 77, 113
health insurance, 10, 11, 58
heat, 22, 23, 29
heating, 26
herbicide, 18
higher quality, 82
hologram, 123
Hong Kong, 42
hormone, 21, 70, 100
hospitals, 11, 31, 58
host, 42
households, 25
hub, 65, 68
human rights, 76
Hungary, 9, 18, 36, 40, 42, 46, 47, 50, 53
hybrid, 58, 59, 61
hydrocarbons, 53, 84

I

identification, 39
IMF, 130
imitation, 12
impact assessment, 26
implants, 21

implementation, 12, 16, 22, 24, 25, 26, 27, 29, 33, 36, 48, 55, 61, 62, 70, 72, 77, 79, 83, 88, 93, 100, 103, 108, 115, 118, 123
import controls, 60
import prices, 4, 81
import restrictions, 72
import substitution, 129
imports, 1, 4, 13, 20, 21, 22, 23, 39, 59, 60, 61, 69, 70, 71, 72, 74, 79, 80, 82, 85, 86, 87, 99, 100, 107, 108, 115, 116, 117, 118, 126, 129, 130, 131, 134
imprisonment, 62, 125
in vitro, 21
incentives, 63, 100, 109
inclusion, 8, 77
income, 101, 104, 126, 134
income tax, 101, 104, 126, 134
incumbents, 44, 48
industry, 8, 9, 10, 11, 15, 16, 18, 28, 32, 36, 37, 38, 39, 40, 41, 42, 44, 54, 61, 63, 82, 83, 84, 85, 87, 88, 92, 94, 96, 97, 100, 101, 113, 117, 118, 121, 122, 123, 125
inefficiency, 67
infectious disease, 94
information sharing, 61
information technology, 55, 79, 80
infrastructure, 31, 32, 63, 67, 92, 94
initiation, 110
innovation, 1, 2, 10, 12, 24, 51
input, 13, 84, 94
inspections, 61, 68, 80, 123, 128
inspectors, 23, 39, 136
institutions, 2, 46, 52, 54, 75
instruments, 4, 76
insurance, 6, 8, 12, 52, 53, 58, 61, 67, 91, 104, 109, 125, 126, 133, 134
integration, 26
intellectual property, 1, 35, 38, 39, 40, 63, 64, 74, 79, 88, 89, 96, 102, 109, 113, 122, 123, 125, 132
intellectual property rights, 1, 35, 38, 40, 64, 74, 79, 88, 89, 96, 102, 109, 122, 125
interference, 133
intermediaries, 6
International Chamber of Commerce, 67, 96
international law, 45, 46
International Monetary Fund, 62
international standards, 85, 118
international trade, vii, 26
interoperability, 30, 74
interpretation, 3, 22, 54
intervention, 99, 134
inventions, 19, 37

investment, 1, 7, 10, 29, 34, 52, 53, 54, 55, 56, 63, 66, 67, 68, 69, 92, 93, 95, 102, 104, 111, 112, 113, 118, 125, 126, 129, 131, 133, 134, 135
investment incentive, 55, 112
investors, 50, 52, 53, 54, 56, 63, 64, 66, 67, 68, 75, 90, 91, 93, 94, 95, 104, 111, 112, 118, 125, 126, 127, 130, 131, 134, 135
IPO, 66
Ireland, 30, 45, 46, 48, 51, 53, 58
ISPs, 65
Italy, 9, 10, 16, 19, 31, 40, 43, 46, 48, 56

J

Japan, 42
joint ventures, 131, 134
judges, 38, 40, 56, 90, 110, 124
judiciary, 40, 68, 128, 134
justification, 13, 24, 70, 72, 87

K

Kazakhstan, 22
Kenya, v, 59, 60, 61, 62, 63, 64, 65, 66, 67, 68
Kyoto protocol, 28

L

labeling, 5, 14, 16, 17, 18, 22, 23, 27, 28, 72, 87, 101, 119, 131
labor, 48, 68, 105, 134, 136
lack of confidence, 124
land, 32, 54, 56, 66, 67, 75, 104, 126, 127
language, vii, 22, 95
Latin America, 6
Latvia, 17, 42
law enforcement, 39, 40, 42, 64, 74, 88, 89, 110, 122
laws, vii, 2, 16, 28, 30, 31, 37, 38, 40, 41, 42, 52, 56, 62, 66, 74, 82, 88, 97, 104, 109, 115, 118, 122, 123, 124, 125, 128, 133, 134
lawyers, 45, 46, 47
layoffs, 77
legal protection, 19, 37, 73, 83
legislation, 7, 8, 9, 11, 18, 19, 20, 21, 24, 26, 27, 30, 35, 36, 37, 38, 39, 40, 41, 42, 43, 44, 46, 48, 51, 53, 54, 55, 63, 72, 73, 87, 88, 89, 90, 94, 101, 102, 108, 110, 111, 112, 115, 119, 124, 125, 126, 127, 133
liberalization, 44, 48, 90, 102, 103, 105, 108
license fee, 92
licenses, vii, 37, 53, 54, 65, 66, 67, 76, 80, 89, 92, 94, 102, 107, 108, 110, 112, 117, 121, 133

Index

light trucks, 78
limitation, 53, 91
limited liability, 46
linkage, 110
Lithuania, 10, 17, 22, 31, 41, 42, 46
litigation, 33, 67, 96, 102
livestock, 20, 100, 107, 108, 120
loans, 34, 67, 133
local authorities, 18, 76, 130
local government, 133
location, 48
logging, 97
long distance, 49, 92
Luxemburg, 49

M

Maastricht Treaty, 52
machinery, 63, 82, 90, 122, 134
magazines, 132
management, 39, 50, 55, 63, 67, 74, 82, 91, 95, 113, 118, 132
manufacturer, 34, 55, 77, 100, 119
manufacturing, 1, 30, 39, 63, 69, 77, 80, 94, 95, 96, 99, 107, 122, 134
market(s), 1, 2, 3, 4, 5, 6, 7, 9, 10, 11, 13, 14, 16, 20, 22, 23, 25, 27, 28, 29, 30, 32, 34, 36, 39, 41, 42, 43, 44, 45, 47, 48, 49, 50, 51, 52, 55, 56, 58, 59, 60, 61, 63, 65, 66, 69, 70, 71, 72, 75, 77, 78, 79, 80, 81, 83, 84, 85, 86, 88, 90, 91, 94, 96, 97, 99, 101, 102, 103, 104, 105, 107, 108, 110, 111, 112, 115, 116, 117, 118, 119, 122, 123, 124, 125, 128, 129, 132
market access, 2, 5, 6, 7, 16, 42, 44, 48, 79, 80, 81, 84, 85, 86, 88, 90, 91, 110, 115, 116, 117, 119, 122, 124, 125
market economics, 128
market position, 11, 50
market segment, 14, 50
market share, 25, 50, 52, 66
market value, 84
marketing, 2, 5, 6, 14, 15, 17, 19, 20, 24, 27, 32, 36, 89, 110, 124
mass media, 54
measures, 6, 7, 9, 10, 12, 13, 15, 17, 20, 26, 27, 35, 36, 39, 44, 53, 55, 56, 60, 73, 78, 79, 85, 88, 94, 102, 108, 109, 118, 119, 121
meat, 13, 22, 70, 71, 100, 108, 130
media, 38, 39, 41, 43, 54, 68, 89, 90, 93, 111, 117, 122, 123
membership, 119, 120
mercury, 25, 26
mergers, 51, 55

metals, 84, 120, 121
Microsoft, 124
middle class, 88
migrants, 56
military, 1, 29, 30, 31, 69, 73, 92, 94, 99
milk, 59, 71, 72
minerals, 23
mining, 56, 69, 75, 134
minority, 53, 56, 93, 95, 113
minors, 43
mobile communication, 51
mobile phone, 49, 50, 51, 66, 92, 127
mobile telecommunication, 66
mobile telephony, 102
models, 4, 32, 34, 112
momentum, 61
money, 30, 31, 82, 135
money laundering, 30
monopoly, 44, 49, 50, 51, 65, 72, 75, 84, 94, 102, 103, 133
moratorium, 14, 15, 18, 100, 101, 127
motion, 38, 41, 73, 87
movement, 52, 96
multimedia, 65
multinational companies, 88
multiplicity, 125
music, 38, 39, 40, 41, 43, 63, 64, 73, 74, 87, 88, 123
music CDs, 88

N

NAFTA, vii
nation, 6, 42, 51, 70, 75, 107
National Health Service, 12
national security, vii, 29, 56, 62, 87, 104
nationality, 47, 75, 76, 125
natural gas, 112, 120
natural resources, 53
negative consequences, 3
negotiating, 79, 96, 115, 129
negotiation, 5, 13
Netherlands, 10, 15, 16, 48
network, 43, 49, 50, 65, 66, 92, 118, 133
New Zealand, 46
newspapers, 132
next generation, 96
NGOs, 15
nickel, 26, 60
North America, vii
North American Free Trade Agreement, vii
Northern Ireland, 46
Norway, v, 69, 70, 71, 72, 73, 74, 75, 76, 77, 78, 104
novelty, 27

O

objectivity, 47
obligation, 3, 5, 16, 37, 44, 122
OECD, 25, 91, 112, 113
offenders, 123
Office of the United States Trade Representative, vii
oil, 60, 76, 84, 94, 95, 101, 104, 112, 120, 122, 130, 134
oil production, 94
oilseed, 17
omission, 46
operator, 16, 43, 49, 50, 51, 66, 75, 95, 102, 133
Operators, 16
organization(s), 6, 18, 28, 34, 64, 73, 74, 93, 120
output, 63
oversight, 104
ownership, 48, 52, 53, 54, 65, 66, 67, 75, 76, 91, 93, 95, 104, 111, 133
ozone, 117

P

Pacific, 6
packaging, 23, 27
parameter, 78
Parliament, 8, 19, 21, 30, 40, 43, 61, 62, 64, 67, 77, 101, 102, 111, 116, 118, 119, 125, 126, 127, 131
partnership(s), 32, 45, 46, 52
pasta, 4, 71, 109
patents, 35, 37, 39, 64, 77, 124
pathogens, 22, 55
patient care, 9
patriotism, 55
payroll, 126
penalties, 18, 35, 38, 41, 62, 64, 88, 89, 90, 94, 109, 110, 122
pensions, 126
perception, 40, 99, 135
performers, 123, 132
permit, 19, 47, 53, 56, 62, 86, 110, 111, 125
pharmaceuticals, 2, 6, 7, 8, 9, 10, 11, 60, 77, 80, 82, 85, 88, 110
piracy, 35, 38, 39, 40, 41, 42, 63, 73, 74, 87, 88, 89, 90, 109, 110, 122, 123, 132
planning, 115, 121
plants, 71, 85, 86, 89, 123
poison, 53, 55
Poland, 10, 19, 20, 36, 41, 42, 48, 51
police, 40, 42, 74, 90, 136
polybrominated biphenyls, 25
polybrominated diphenyl ethers, 25
polycarbonate, 122
pools, 104
poor, 61, 108, 125, 135
population, 93, 96, 105, 127
port of entry, 61, 68, 82
ports, 68, 72, 121
Portugal, 11, 20, 31, 36, 37, 48
potato, 100
poultry, 2, 4, 13, 20, 21, 22, 80, 85, 86, 107, 108, 116, 118
power, 26, 36, 49, 67, 75, 83, 94, 104, 105, 112, 135
power generation, 94, 112
power plants, 83
predictability, 12, 70, 81
preference, 76, 88, 92, 109, 120
preferential treatment, 95
prejudice, 53
premiums, 133
pressure, 7, 8, 14, 32, 50
prestige, 45
prevention, 43
prices, 6, 7, 8, 9, 10, 11, 12, 34, 49, 51, 81, 82, 83, 84, 102, 105, 107, 109, 121, 132
pricing policies, 7, 8
privacy, 56, 74
private enterprises, 112
private investment, 111
private sector, 60, 61, 67, 111
privatization, 30, 43, 65, 67, 75, 76, 102, 108, 112, 127
probe, 50
producers, 9, 11, 13, 14, 16, 17, 18, 20, 22, 25, 33, 34, 36, 40, 70, 72, 80, 84, 87, 89, 100, 113, 117, 121, 122, 123, 132
product life cycle, 26
production, 2, 6, 17, 18, 19, 20, 21, 22, 25, 28, 29, 32, 33, 34, 39, 53, 55, 70, 71, 76, 83, 88, 89, 90, 93, 94, 100, 101, 105, 111, 112, 117, 121, 122, 123, 124, 130
profession(s), 45, 54, 111
profit(s), 7, 12, 76, 94, 95, 112, 118, 126, 134
program, 9, 15, 27, 33, 34, 61, 63, 68, 83, 85, 101, 122, 123
programming, 43, 103
property rights, 35, 38, 64, 88, 93, 97
protocol, 16, 50
public affairs, 14
public awareness, 41, 73
public financing, 33
public health, 7, 8, 24, 58, 77, 108
public interest, 48
public radio, 43
public sector, 76

publishers, 40
PVC, 61

Q

qualifications, 46
quality control, 61
quotas, vii, 3, 4, 5, 13, 43, 44, 70, 71, 72, 79, 80, 99, 100, 121, 130

R

radio, 43, 44, 74, 75, 92, 125
range, 16, 28, 31, 34, 46, 54, 70, 90, 92, 107, 118, 120
rape, 17
rate of return, 9, 34
raw materials, 39, 59, 60, 63, 71, 122
reactants, 118
real estate, 53, 54, 56, 76
reciprocity, 53
recognition, 1, 14, 54, 64, 111, 122
reconcile, 2
recovery, 27, 83
recycling, 25, 26
reduction, 10, 71, 81, 123
reforms, 7, 86, 113
regulation(s), vii, 2, 5, 8, 9, 10, 12, 13, 16, 17, 18, 19, 20, 21, 22, 23, 24, 27, 28, 29, 30, 38, 41, 43, 44, 45, 47, 48, 49, 50, 52, 55, 56, 57, 59, 61, 63, 69, 71, 72, 75, 77, 82, 84, 85, 88, 90, 92, 93, 99, 100, 101, 103, 108, 110, 111, 117, 118, 119, 122, 125, 128, 130, 131, 132, 133, 134, 136
regulators, 47, 48, 91, 105
regulatory framework, 19, 48, 55, 65, 75, 134
reinsurance, 104, 133
rejection, 16
relationship, 1, 6, 14, 129
reliability, 16
rent, 76
repair, 94
replacement, 23, 36, 70
reputation, 121
reserves, 62, 129
resistance, 100
resolution, 5, 13, 67, 90, 93, 120, 126, 135
resources, 53, 74, 118
restaurants, 135
restructuring, 65, 96
retail, 7, 11, 38, 39, 41, 72, 76, 82, 83, 85, 123, 124, 129, 130
returns, 76

revenue, 44, 64, 76, 77, 105, 130
rice, 2, 4, 15, 59, 87, 108
risk, 19, 20, 21, 24, 57, 58, 61, 67, 72, 83, 86, 87, 108, 119, 128
risk assessment, 21, 61, 72, 86, 119
rods, 13
Romania, 2, 3, 4, 20, 22, 23, 28, 41, 56
royalty, 123
rule of law, 135
Russia, v, 13, 38, 79, 80, 81, 82, 83, 84, 85, 86, 87, 88, 89, 90, 91, 92, 93, 94, 95, 96, 97

S

safety, 15, 24, 82, 118, 136
sales, 1, 8, 11, 12, 20, 23, 34, 37, 55, 63, 69, 72, 78, 82, 88, 94, 99, 107, 110, 113, 119, 124
salmon, 116, 119
salmonella, 22
sanctions, 21, 29, 122
satellite, 73, 92
savings, 10
scientific community, 17
search, 131, 132
security(ies), 1, 18, 54, 56, 60, 62, 67, 68, 70, 91, 93, 104, 117, 128
seed, 16, 17, 18, 19, 20, 59, 61, 72, 101
seizure, 90, 123, 131
Senate, 18
sentencing, 125
separation, 16
series, 1, 22, 57, 94, 101
service provider, 44, 48, 50, 52, 102, 125
shape, 6
shareholders, 53, 54, 55, 56, 66, 95, 113, 127, 134
shares, 30, 55, 56, 66, 67, 77, 94, 102
sharing, 13, 39, 42, 48, 73
sheep, 4, 121
shelter, 70
shortage, 111, 116, 121
signals, 41
signs, 40
single market, 6, 56, 69
sites, 38, 42, 89, 127
Slovakia, 11, 46, 47
smuggling, 126
social security, 8, 30
Social Security, 9
society, 99
software, 41, 63, 82, 87, 89, 97, 123, 127
solvency, 104
solvents, 28, 83
South Africa, 61, 67

South Asia, vii, 63
soybean(s) 19, 20, 72, 99, 119
Spain, 11, 16, 20, 23, 32, 33, 41, 44, 48, 51
speculation, 95
speech, 128
sports, 96
stability, 111
stages, 119
stakeholders, 10, 12, 13, 14, 39, 41, 85
standardization, 14, 118, 131
standards, 8, 13, 14, 17, 23, 26, 27, 28, 29, 61, 78, 85, 102, 113, 118, 119, 126, 131
starch, 17
state aid, 34
statistics, 29, 74, 133
steel, vii, 28, 60, 84, 121, 127
stock, 1, 55, 56, 59, 69, 76, 79, 99, 107, 115, 129
stock exchange, 76
storage, 121
students, 54
subjectivity, 12
subscribers, 51, 66
subsidization, 14
subsidy, 9, 33, 34, 83
substitutes, 7
substitution, 8
sugar, 34, 60, 81, 109, 111, 116
sulphur, 28
summer, 18, 44, 116
supervision, 103
suppliers, 5, 6, 16, 29, 30, 34, 70, 83, 86, 87, 90, 92, 101
supply, 7, 11, 16, 33, 59, 60, 76, 91, 121
supply chain, 16
Supreme Court, 90
surplus, 59, 99, 107
surprise, 123
suspensions, 89
sustainable development, 72
sustainable economic growth, 128
Sweden, 22, 42, 48
Switzerland, v, 57, 69, 99, 100, 101, 102, 103, 104, 105
systems, 25, 26, 29, 30, 47, 55, 66, 73, 86, 92, 100, 108, 118, 125

T

tactics, 56
takeover, 52, 55, 56
Tanzania, 59, 67
targets, 26, 27
tariff, vii, 2, 3, 4, 5, 20, 59, 60, 69, 70, 79, 80, 81, 82, 99, 100, 107, 108, 116, 117
tariff rates, 3, 69, 81, 99, 107, 116
tax base, 81, 126
tax collection, 94
tax credit, 109
tax evasion, 126
tax rates, 111, 130
tax reform(s), 94, 126
taxation, 52, 78, 93, 133, 134
technology, 8, 17, 29, 34, 55, 65, 80, 94, 97, 109, 126
technology transfer, 109
telecommunications, 29, 31, 48, 49, 50, 51, 55, 65, 67, 75, 80, 84, 91, 92, 102, 110, 125, 128, 133
Telecommunications Act, 49, 50, 102
telecommunications services, 48, 75, 92, 110, 133
telephone, 49, 65, 66, 75, 92, 102
television, 43, 44, 49, 50, 75, 93, 125
territory, 93
tertiary education, 54
test data, 36, 88, 109, 110, 124
textiles, 24, 130
theft, 40
theory, vii, 2, 127
threat, 12, 130
threshold(s), 16, 19, 30, 58, 62, 73, 75, 101, 103, 109, 122
timber, 97
time, 3, 8, 13, 15, 16, 18, 42, 43, 62, 67, 74, 75, 78, 80, 81, 82, 84, 85, 86, 92, 94, 96, 99, 100, 102, 119, 120, 131, 133, 135
time frame, 86
tobacco, 41, 60, 108
total revenue, 43
tourism, 63
toxic substances, 55
toxicity, 100
trade, vii, 1, 2, 3, 5, 6, 7, 13, 14, 16, 20, 21, 22, 23, 24, 27, 34, 38, 39, 44, 53, 59, 61, 64, 67, 68, 69, 70, 71, 79, 80, 82, 83, 84, 85, 86, 93, 97, 99, 100, 101, 103, 107, 108, 115, 116, 118, 119, 121, 122, 129, 130, 131, 132, 135
trade deficit, 1, 69, 79, 99, 107, 115, 129
trade policies, 69
trade policy, 2, 129
trade union, 103
trade war, vii
trademarks, 35, 37, 40, 64, 88, 96, 124
trading, 6, 24, 79, 108, 112
trading partners, 24, 108
traffic, 65
training, 46, 132

transaction value, 60
transactions, 93, 96, 113, 135
transition, 22, 91
transition period, 22, 91
transmission, 43, 57, 75, 94, 105, 110, 112, 133
transparency, 6, 8, 9, 10, 11, 12, 13, 14, 29, 31, 54, 62, 77, 78, 87, 89, 92, 94, 108, 113, 120, 125, 131, 132, 134
transport, 21, 29, 52, 56
transportation, 29, 60, 104, 111
transshipment, 22, 38
treaties, 52, 109
trend, 40, 94
trial, 81
trust, 51
Turkey, v, 38, 107, 108, 109, 110, 111, 112, 113
turnover, 7, 103

U

UK, 12, 32, 34, 48, 53
Ukraine, v, 38, 115, 116, 117, 118, 119, 120, 121, 122, 123, 124, 125, 126, 127, 128
uncertainty, 5, 10, 14, 25, 49, 111
UNESCO, 103
uniform, 2, 3
unions, 3, 105
United Kingdom, 12, 32, 34
United Nations, 67, 111, 121, 134
United States, 1, 2, 3, 4, 5, 6, 13, 14, 15, 19, 20, 21, 22, 23, 24, 26, 27, 28, 29, 30, 32, 33, 34, 35, 36, 37, 38, 40, 42, 43, 44, 47, 53, 57, 69, 70, 77, 78, 79, 80, 81, 82, 83, 84, 85, 86, 87, 88, 89, 90, 91, 99, 100, 102, 107, 108, 111, 115, 116, 119, 120, 121, 122, 123, 124, 125, 129, 133, 135
universities, 31, 54
uranium, 13
Uruguay, 70
Uruguay Round, 70
USDA, 15
users, 42, 50, 65, 96, 105, 127
Uzbekistan, v, 129, 130, 131, 132, 133, 134, 135

V

validation, 25
validity, 92, 124

values, 25, 73, 109
VAT, 48, 59, 60, 63, 80, 81, 82, 94, 108, 116, 117, 126, 134
vegetables, 4, 70, 107, 116
vehicles, 36, 78, 81, 113, 116, 117
vertical integration, 84
vitamins, 23
voice, 48, 50, 75, 133
voters, 100, 101, 103
voting, 53, 56, 67

W

wage payments, 126
Wales, 46
warrants, 55
weapons, 76
websites, 41, 73, 87, 88, 96, 123, 127, 128
Western Europe, 40
wheat, 4, 18, 59, 60, 99, 109, 121
wholesale, 1, 49, 51, 75, 80, 83, 99, 107, 129
windows, 27
wine, 5, 13, 14, 34, 72, 81, 88, 108, 117
winning, 92
withdrawal, 34
wood, 15, 23, 34, 84, 97
wood products, 15, 84
workers, 1
workplace, 104
World Bank, 30, 62, 121
World Trade Organization, 42, 59, 79, 100, 108, 115, 129
writing, 28, 134
WTO, 1, 3, 4, 5, 6, 10, 13, 14, 15, 19, 20, 21, 23, 28, 32, 33, 34, 35, 38, 42, 48, 59, 60, 62, 63, 70, 73, 79, 80, 81, 82, 83, 84, 85, 86, 87, 88, 89, 90, 91, 100, 101, 108, 109, 110, 115, 116, 117, 118, 119, 120, 121, 122, 124, 125, 126, 129, 132

Y

yield, 81